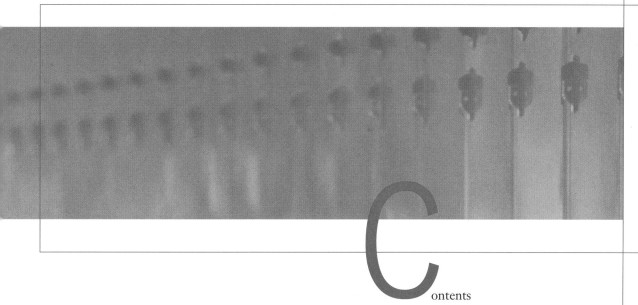

Contents

A Guide for Those Who Care About Creating and Supporting **Quality in Schools**

Leading Learning Communities

NAESP
Standards for What

Principals
Should
Know
and Be Able
To Do

National Association of Elementary School Principals

National Association of Elementary School Principals
Serving Elementary and Middle School Principals
in their commitment to Our Children – Our Schools – Our Future.

Leading Learning Communities: Standards for What Principals Should Know and Be Able To Do was created by the National Association of Elementary School Principals in partnership with Collaborative Communications Group.

The research and development of this document was made possible by the LAB at Brown University, Principals Leadership Network, funded by the Office of Educational Research and Improvement, U.S. Department of Education.

Funds for the publication were generously contributed by Lifetouch, Inc., of Minneapolis, Paul Harmel, President and Chief Executive Officer.

National Association of Elementary School Principals
1615 Duke Street
Alexandria, VA 22314-3483
Phone: 800-38-NAESP
Fax: 800-39-NAESP
Email: naesp@naesp.org
Web site: www.naesp.org

The 28,500 members of the National Association of Elementary School Principals provide administrative and instructional leadership for public and private elementary and middle schools throughout the United States, Canada and overseas. Founded in 1921, NAESP is an independent professional association with its own headquarters building in Alexandria, Virginia. Through national and regional meetings, award-winning publications and joint efforts with its 50 state affiliates, NAESP is a strong advocate for both its members and for the 33 million American children enrolled in preschool, kindergarten and grades 1 through 8.

Executive Director: Vincent L. Ferrandino, Ed.D.
Deputy Executive Director: Gail Connelly Gross
Deputy Executive Director: Deborah B. Reeve, Ed.D.
Associate Executive Director, Professional Services: Fred Brown

---

Collaborative Communications Group
1801 Connecticut Avenue, N.W.
Third Floor
Washington, DC 20009
Phone: 202-986-4959
Fax: 202-986-4958
Email: info@publicengagement.com
Web site: www.publicengagement.com

Collaborative Communications Group is a strategic communications consulting firm built around the belief that public engagement is essential to the improvement of communities and, particularly, schools. Collaborative Communications Group works in three portfolio areas: defining and analyzing the nature and impact of civic engagement in the context of organization, education and community change; developing tools to increase and improve the practice of engagement; and improving the management and communications capacity of organizations that serve as primary initiators or supporters of engagement activities.

ISBN 0-939327-15-5

Foreword By Dr. Vincent Ferrandino

Improving Schools Requires New Thinking About School Leadership

The idea of principal as instructional leader isn't new. Nor is it new to think of supporting principals in their lead teaching role. Indeed, a *Principal* magazine article suggested that "most principals may be finding it more difficult than ever to act the part of 'teacher of teachers.'" The same article stated: "There seems to be a tendency to depict the principal as a man [sic] increasingly bypassed and forgotten, losing status as the school's instructional leader." That was in 1965.

What is new? With *Leading Learning Communities: What Principals Should Know and Be Able To Do*, the National Association of Elementary School Principals (NAESP) is taking a fresh look at the role of school leader. Influenced by the academic standards movement — which is demanding that we focus on equity and instruction as never before — school leaders are thinking anew about how to define "quality" in schools and how to create and manage the environments that support it.

For years, NAESP has periodically updated two documents, *Standards for Quality Elementary & Middle Schools* and *Proficiencies for Principals*. This year, we've merged them into one. We wanted to create a tangible and physical representation of our belief that the two ambitions are inextricably linked: You cannot have a first-rate school without first-rate school leadership. And regardless of how charismatic or personable a school leader is, or how effective a manager, a principal is not going to improve academic achievement for all students unless she engages in her work differently.

Everything a principal does in school must be focused on ensuring the learning of students and adults.

Although long seen as essential forces in school change, principals have been largely absent from conversations defining their own role as school leaders. In this guide, principals outline what their role in school improvement can and should be.

In *Leading Learning Communities*, principals themselves identify six characteristics of instructional leadership. These characteristics are portrayed in the form of Standards for Principals. The standards relate to the Indicators of Quality in Schools.

Standards are driving new thinking about student — and adult — learning. This in turn is forcing us to rethink not only the way we see the role of principal as leader, but also the way we see the role of principal as manager. The myriad management responsibilities a principal faces don't go away. But the framework for how schools are managed needs to change: Everything a principal does in school (whether observing instruction or ordering materials) must be focused on ensuring the learning of students and adults.

With this guide, we're taking the opportunity to look anew at the role of leadership in schools. Clearly, we don't have all the answers. But we do have some answers. This guide is an important step in helping principals move toward new thinking and new behavior.

Over the next few years, NAESP will be looking deeply into new models of leadership — and sharing effective strategies and practices along the way. Without new thinking about the way schools are run, we will likely see continuous change but very little real improvement.

Dr. Vincent Ferrandino is executive director of the National Association of Elementary School Principals (NAESP).

In this document:

- Principals publicly state their belief that all students — regardless of race, gender or socioeconomic status — are entitled to a high-quality education. Furthermore, principals take responsibility for creating shared commitment to that vision in their school communities. They hold academic departments responsible for results. They take responsibility for monitoring and implementing curriculum and instruction to ensure equity.

- Principals recognize the balance between their work as manager and that of leader. In addition, principals position themselves as learners. The linchpin in the delivery of accountability and support for professional development, principals take responsibility for their own professional development.

- Principals say that data is a tool for decision-making about improving instruction, not a vehicle to identify and punish schools that aren't making the grade.

- Principals emphasize that unless citizens fulfill their civic responsibility to ensure quality, public schools are not likely to improve dramatically. Furthermore, principals take responsibility for actively engaging parents, business leaders and others in the community to participate in new forms of decision-making and shared accountability.

- Finally, principals call for authority to be aligned with responsibility. In the last section of this guide, principals recommend new sources of support (at the federal, state, district and community levels) that will enable greater autonomy and authority. For instance, to be truly effective leaders of school learning communities, principals need to have the ability to hire and fire teachers, to implement curriculum and assessments relevant to state standards and school learning goals and to purchase resources they deem appropriate and necessary.

How To Use This Guide

Leading Learning Communities: Standards for What Principals Should Know and Be Able To Do

Leading Learning Communities is a guide to help principals reflect on — thus improve — their practice. We hope that others interested in school improvement will use it too, whether they are school board members, superintendents, professors of education, teachers or parents. We didn't create this guide to be used by policymakers as an assessment tool for principals. This is a resource for principals to help them improve their work and their schools.

We've designed this guide to draw direct connections between the quality of schools and the role of the school leader. Because high-quality schools are inextricably linked to the action of school leaders, we connected them. We start by identifying indicators of what we believe constitutes quality in school, and then we define six standards for what school leaders must know and do to reach those indicators. The standards cannot be implemented piecemeal. To be successful, principals need to integrate them. Think of the standards as a recipe for good schools, not as a menu from which to pick and choose.

We've designed the guide to encourage those who care about building knowledge and skills. This guide is all about instructional leadership. But you won't find one particular section devoted to that topic. Nor will you find any one section on the management responsibilities of the principal. This is intentional: We believe that instructional leadership and management responsibilities focused on student learning permeate each of the six standards.

We've designed this guide to reflect the voices of the principals who helped develop these ideas. No one speaks with more authority about school leadership than principals themselves. Principals are honest, compelling spokespeople about the challenges and opportunities in their profession. The Voices of Principals comments throughout this guide come from an online learning community of principals organized for the creation of this document.

We've designed the guide to show that the concepts outlined here really work. Each chapter includes stories of real people in real schools that exemplify the ideas outlined in this guide. We've given these stories a name: Focus on Practice. We expect the readers of this guide to come from all kinds of schools, so we've used examples across a wide geographic and demographic spectrum.

We've designed the guide to encourage reflection and self-examination. Each standards section contains a list of practical guiding questions principals can ask themselves or a small group, at faculty meetings or with grade- or subject-level teams. Self-assessments are included at the end of each section to help you think about where your strengths are and where you might need additional attention. These assessments are aligned with the standards and the indicators of quality in schools. It's all connected.

We've designed the book to invite browsing. Readers may want to refer back to particular standards as a reference. So we've created distinct sections for each of the six standards. Each section contains specific strategies to help meet the standard, along with references to the research that supports our conclusions. In addition, each section contains Tools and NAESP Resources to help you.

Remember, the mantra of effective leaders of learning communities is: I am not here as someone who has everything figured out, but rather as one who struggles. One never "arrives" at the place where they know how to be principal. The role itself is an exercise in the on-the-job training. We hope this guide helps you identify what you need for your ongoing professional development.

Introduction

The Need for an Expanded Role for Principals

It may seem obvious that schools should be focused on learning. But the truth of the matter is that some students learn and progress, and some don't. Our collective experience has led us to believe that the most effective way to get all students to perform at higher levels in a short period of time requires agreed-upon standards for what they should know and be able to do.

The concept of standards — academic standards for students and professional standards for what constitutes quality in teaching — has broad appeal. Educators, policymakers, parents, business leaders and others seem to like the notion of making public our expectations for students and adults, and then holding people accountable to those expectations. The atmosphere of high-stakes accountability and testing has created significant political pressure to deliver on the standards movement's promise of improved student achievement.

The academic standards movement also has amplified the call for improved instruction. Student achievement is at the center of the national dialogue about the effectiveness — indeed, the viability — of public schools. We've learned that it's meaningless to set high expectations for student performance unless we also set high expectations for the performance of adults. We know that if we are going to improve learning, we must also improve teaching. And we must improve the environment in which teaching and learning occur.

Elementary and middle school principals are essential to helping students reach standards. The business of schools has changed. Principals can no longer simply be administrators and managers. They must be leaders in improving instruction and student achievement. They must be the force that creates collaboration and cohesion around school learning goals and the commitment to achieve those goals.

No longer can a principal be judged solely on how well he or she manages the administrative duties of a school. The quality of the principal must relate to a school's capacity to ensure achievement for all children.

Six Standards That Characterize Instructional Leadership

With the help of principals throughout the association, NAESP has identified six standards for what principals should know and be able to do. These actions, taken together, serve as our definition of what constitutes instructional leadership. Effective leaders:

- **Lead schools in a way that places student and adult learning at the center.**

- **Set high expectations and standards for the academic and social development of all students and the performance of adults.**

- **Demand content and instruction that ensure student achievement of agreed-upon academic standards.**

- **Create a culture of continuous learning for adults tied to student learning and other school goals.**

- **Use multiple sources of data as diagnostic tools to assess, identify and apply instructional improvement.**

- **Actively engage the community to create shared responsibility for student and school success.**

Creating new models of school leadership will require changes in practice. Student learning must be at the center of what schools are all about and should drive all the decisions school leaders make. Principals themselves must reflect on the way they work.

To accomplish this, the organizations principals serve and that serve them must support principals' professional growth. NAESP must demonstrate bold and steady leadership that positions student and adult learning at the center of school leadership. We intend to provide additional professional development opportunities and other resources that will support that expanded role.

This guide is a first step.

Indicators of Quality in Schools

There is a lot of discussion these days about providing a "high-quality education for all students." But "quality" means different things to different people. Before schools can deliver high-quality curriculum, instruction and learning experiences, we must first define what we mean by quality in the first place. The following indicators represent what NAESP believes defines quality in schools. Talk to your staff about this list. How many of these indicators are present in your school? Are there others you would add?

Leadership that places student and adult learning at the center of schools

Having a first-rate school without first-rate leadership is impossible. Leadership is a balance of management and vision. There is simply no way a principal alone can perform all the complex tasks of a school. Responsibility must be distributed, and people must understand the values behind various tasks. A full-time, qualified school leader places student and adult learning at the center of all decisions in a school. In addition, effective leadership requires that principals have the autonomy to make decisions based on needs of individual schools. Effective leadership also depends on having the authority to hold people accountable to results.

Expectations for and commitment to high standards of academic performance

All members of the school community must commit to a common vision of the school and to high academic standards. All people in the school must be clear about what students are expected to learn and what teachers are expected to teach. If people in the school do not believe that all children are capable of learning at high levels, then some children will continue to fall through the cracks. If all of the people in the school do not see it as their responsibility to move children to higher levels of performance, then children simply will not get there.

Safe and secure learning environments for students

Beyond rigorous academics, students need a balance of emotional and personal supports. Schools should provide common areas of learning, knowledge and skills and understanding that allow children to function in society. Students need to know that someone cares about them in school. Students should feel safe at school — whether on the grounds of the school, in the crosswalk, or in the classroom. They should enjoy coming to school, as a place to build social relationships and to develop personal skills and attributes. In addition, their learning environments must engage them.

Curriculum and instruction tied to school and student learning goals

Successful schools are organized around student learning. Schools that support these expectations set priorities for what teachers teach and what students learn. And they provide a sufficient number of well-qualified personnel to meet school goals. Schools that achieve high levels of student performance provide the resources and supports that ensure student success. Recognizing that all students do not learn at the same pace, schools that support student success give students the time they need to meet high academic standards. In addition, these schools provide rigorous curricula and the instructional strategies that support all students, particularly those who are low-performing. Classroom observation, continual evaluation of teaching practice and review and analysis of student work also ensure equity in the learning of all students. In addition, schools that are deliberate about raising the performance of all students regularly collect, study and analyze data to improve decision-making about instruction and student learning.

Collaborative learning community for adults

If adults don't learn, then students won't learn either. No matter how good school goals are, they cannot be met if the school isn't organized to accomplish them. The school operates as a learning community that uses its own experience and knowledge, and that of others, to improve the performance of students and teachers alike. Continuous school improvement planning must be based on improved student learning. Instructional practices must be aligned with high standards. Teachers and other adults in the school must receive open, honest and fair communication when they are observed and evaluated. Schools that learn have a climate that encourages the capabilities and emphasizes the worth of individuals. They must be a place where learning isn't isolated, where adults demonstrate their care about kids but also care about each other. In such places, learning takes place in groups. A culture of shared responsibility is established, and everybody learns from one another.

An engaged community

Engaged parents, business leaders, members of the neighborhood and other taxpaying citizens may not be essential to student success — but they sure help! All of these people have a stake in the success of the school and the students in it. Thus, school goals must be communicated not just to those who work in school but to the community as well. Schools must have open and honest communication — a willingness to tell the bad along with the good. In addition, they must provide a warm, non-threatening environment that welcomes community involvement. Those with a stake in the school should have the opportunity to share in the decisions that affect them. This might include the opportunity to support appropriate funding for the school, mentor students, participate on school improvement or site-based decision-making teams, or show support for school activities. In addition, community support systems for the school, including volunteers and business and parent support should be welcomed and utilized.

Defining Instructional Leadership

Six Standards for What Principals Should Know and Be Able To Do and Strategies for Achieving Them

STANDARD ONE: Lead schools in a way that places student and adult learning at the center.

STRATEGIES:

- Create and foster a community of learners

- Embody learner-centered leadership

- Seek leadership contributions from multiple sources

- Tie the daily operations of the schoolhouse to school and student learning goals

STANDARD TWO: Set high expectations and standards for the academic and social development of all students and the performance of adults.

STRATEGIES:

- Articulate a clear vision that reflects the beliefs, values and commitments of the school community

- Ensure that all students have adequate and appropriate opportunities to meet high standards

- Develop a school culture that is flexible, collaborative, innovative and supportive of efforts to improve achievement of all students

STANDARD THREE: Demand content and instruction that ensure student achievement of agreed-upon academic standards.

STRATEGIES:

- Hire and retain high-quality teachers and hold them responsible for student learning

- Monitor alignment of curriculum with standards, school goals and assessments

- Observe classroom practices to assure that all students are meaningfully engaged in active learning

- Provide up-to-date technology and instructional materials

- Review and analyze student work to determine whether students are being taught to standard

STANDARD FOUR: Create a culture of continuous learning for adults tied to student learning and other school goals.

STRATEGIES:

- Provide time for reflection as an important part of improving practice

- Invest in teacher learning

- Connect professional development to school learning goals

- Provide opportunities for teachers to work, plan and think together

- Recognize the need to continually improve principals' own professional practice

STANDARD FIVE: Use multiple sources of data as diagnostic tools to assess, identify and apply instructional improvement.

STRATEGIES:

- Consider a variety of data sources to measure performance

- Analyze data using a variety of strategies

- Use data as tools to identify barriers to success, design strategies for improvement and plan daily instruction

- Benchmark successful schools with similar demographics to identify strategies for improving student achievement

- Create a school environment that is comfortable using data

STANDARD SIX: Actively engage the community to create shared responsibility for student and school success.

STRATEGIES:

- Engage the community to build greater ownership for the work of the school

- Share leadership and decision-making

- Encourage parents to become meaningfully involved in the school and in their own children's learning

- Ensure that students and families are connected to the health, human and social services they need to stay focused on learning

1 Leadership | **2** Vision | **3** Student Learning | **4** Adult Learning | **5** Data & Decision-Making | **6** Community Engagement

9

Standard One: Balance Management and Leadership Roles

Effective principals lead schools in a way that places student and adult learning at the center.

Schools, as representations of our larger society, are places of continual change. Many of these changes represent both serious challenges and wonderful opportunities:

- The growing diversity in our communities and schools adds a richness to the daily experience, but also stretches our capacity to address the needs of all children. The achievement gap of poor and minority populations continues to lag despairingly behind that of their more affluent counterparts.

- Vast leaps in technological change open new horizons and, at the same time, demand new learning.

- The academic standards movement is driving a focus on instruction. It is also creating a public backlash that is potentially a serious weapon against public schools that fail to help their students reach the standards.

Societal change is now so far-reaching that no amount of education can prepare adults to meet the demands that will be made on them. That reality is driving schools to prepare upcoming generations for their futures as lifelong learners; it is fundamentally changing the way society thinks about teaching and learning.

We do know that if we keep doing things the way we always have, we'll keep getting the same results. Thus, schools themselves require continual learning. Our notion of school leaders is also changing, requiring all leaders to focus on both instructional and managerial tasks.

The new model of a school leader is one who is continually learning. The leader's task is allowing people throughout the organization to deal productively with the critical issues they face and to develop mastery in learning disciplines.

Principals' Voices:

"Part of the principal's role is to manage. But, more importantly, the principal needs to lead and help all members to become leaders."

In "Making Sense As a School Leader," authors Ackerman, Donaldson and Van Der Bogert write that leaders "who embrace open inquiry, the sharing of problems and solutions, and collective responsibility will foster creativity, resourcefulness and collaboration in the work of staff and the learning of children." These characteristics are the earmarks of leaders who seek to learn and to invent through questioning.

On the other hand, it is possible to see the role of principal as not so different from what it was before. After all, principals are still responsible for matters such as school safety, maintenance, fire drills, facilities and scheduling. They still must ensure that people get paid and that the buses get children home on time.

Learning how to balance these roles isn't something taught in university programs. And moving up from teacher to principal doesn't automatically mean that new skills and sensibilities come with the title.

The trick is not to do more, but to rethink how and why you're doing what you're doing. And to keep a simple concept in mind: Everything a principal does in school should be focused on ensuring the learning of both students and adults.

What would it look like if principals were balancing these management and leadership roles successfully? We would see principals who:

> - **Create and foster a community of learners**
>
> - **Embody learner-centered leadership**
>
> - **Seek leadership contributions from multiple sources**
>
> - **Tie the daily operations of the schoolhouse to school and student learning goals**

Create and foster a community of learners

Central to our concept of high-quality schools is the creation of learning communities. The notion of schools as learning communities is growing because it must. Schools must be places where everyone in them — adults as well as students — is continually learning and developing.

Throughout this guide, we use the phrases "learning community" and "community of learners" interchangeably. What we mean is this: School must be a place where students and adults alike are responsible not only for student learning but for their own learning and that of their colleagues. Behind this definition is the belief that when adults stop learning, so do students.

Principals' Voices:

"The principalship is really a profession of opportunities."

1 Leadership | **2** Vision | **3** Student Learning | **4** Adult Learning | **5** Data & Decision-Making | **6** Community Engagement

11

The goal of learning communities is to build social and intellectual connections among people. Control interferes with the process. The leader of a learning community is a "developmentalist," someone who knows where he or she stands on the issues and is committed to growth over time.

Focus on Practice:

Improving Instruction With Strong Management
Newman Elementary School, Montana

Some principals see the management of the school and academic instruction as two distinct things. But at Newman Elementary School in Billings, Montana, effective classroom instruction is intertwined with strong management.

Principal Darrell Rud views his management responsibilities for hiring, budgeting and scheduling as essential to the academic success of the school.

Rud ensures that teachers know the important skills — or standards — that children are expected to achieve, and that they are equipped with the professional development tools and resources to do it. For example, on Tuesdays, teachers have extra time when students leave early to focus visioning and planning. These sessions emphasize forward-thinking and collaboration.

Providing flexibility to teachers in how they help students meet standards is important. "You need to get the right people in the right positions," Rud said. "While clearly defining what needs to be taught, you must be flexible on how it is taught."

When budgeting, Rud focuses on aligning resources with instructional goals. For the 300 students — nearly one-third of whom are Native American or Hispanic — it means that math is a core focus of budget allocation. At the Title I school, the alignment also includes assessment tools, whereby teachers and parents are assured that the school is doing what it says it will instructionally.

Scheduling at Newman is done with "creativity and prioritization." By knowing his staff and their abilities, Rud is able to use his school's human resources to their fullest potential, maximizing the amount of time adults spend in the classroom.

"The principal represents the heart and soul of every public school in America."

Jonathan Kozol,
NAESP convention
San Diego (2001)

Embody learner-centered leadership

Leadership is a learning activity. By allowing ourselves to see leaders as learners, we create a new image of principals' work, and we present the principal as a model learner. Indeed, the image of principal is one of a public learner. Public learning can be a powerful model for everyone in the school community. Put simply, if children are to be resourceful, energetic and responsible for their own learning, so must every adult in the school — especially the principal. In ever-changing schools, being principal is akin to being the chief learning officer. Through a careful mix of teamwork, assessment, reflection and inspiration, the principal leads the school — managerially, instructionally and motivationally.

Seek leadership contributions from multiple sources

Leaders acknowledge that different types of expertise exist at different levels of the school. The ability to draw on different people where that knowledge is distributed is what Richard Elmore calls "distributed leadership." The basic idea is simple: People in any organization or system develop specialties that reflect their interests, aptitudes and skills. At the same time, even people in similar roles will have different levels of competence.

Harnessing these varied talents so that they complement each other is a skill and an art. Equally challenging is the work of figuring out when there is enough competence within the school to solve its own problems, and when outside help is needed. Schools are places of knowledge-intensive enterprises such as teaching and learning. There is simply no way a principal alone can perform all of the complex tasks in a school. Responsibility for leadership must be distributed. And a common culture must be created to make this distribution meaningful. How and why leadership gets distributed hold together a team on a common task and help people understand the values behind the task.

To help balance the demands of running a successful school, today's principal maximizes the talents and skills of other adults in the school by promoting a shared leadership team. By utilizing assistant principals or other administrators and teacher leaders to handle issues such as the physical plant, social services, discipline and personnel, the principal broadens school attention and resources to such issues. By using teacher leaders to aid in curriculum issues, data collection, professional development and school safety issues, the principal provides the classroom teacher with a greater stake in the success and direction of the school.

This shared leadership not only provides greater coverage and attention to school needs, but it also plays a valuable role in developing skills and cultivating abilities to the school leaders of tomorrow. By dividing duties and tasks, and delegating realms of responsibility, principals demonstrate true leadership by maximizing all of the resources available to them.

The principal doesn't have to do it all, but he or she is responsible for getting it done.

Wanted: School Leaders

Large numbers of today's principals are reaching retirement age, and research suggests a steady decline in the number of qualified candidates for openings at every level. Indeed, schools are facing a dangerous shortage of school leaders. To strengthen and maintain the quality of the profession, principals can:

- Educate the school community on the duties and demands of today's principal
- Promote community understanding of both the managerial and leadership requirements of the position
- Provide mentoring support to new and prospective principals; and
- Encourage talented educators to consider the principalship

Source: *The Principal, Keystone of a High-Achieving School: Attracting and Keeping the Leaders We Need.* Arlington, VA: Educational Research Service, 2000.

Principals' Voices:

"I found that virtually everything that I do on a regular or spontaneous basis affects the quality of instruction and degree of learning that takes place within the school."

Focus on Practice:

Community of Learners, Community of Leaders
South Houston Elementary School, Texas

Leadership is a shared responsibility at South Houston Elementary School. At this urban Texas school, teachers are encouraged to be a part of the leadership team. Principal Karen Holt has created a system that cultivates every staff member's leadership potential.

As part of this effort, Title I funds are used to pay some teachers as "peer facilitators," who spend 60 percent of their time with students and the remaining 40 percent with other teachers. This mix provides opportunities for identifying and developing skills, gaining confidence and promoting a sense of "we" in the classroom. Each peer facilitator is empowered to lead a topic in the school. For example, one facilitator might focus on technology, leading the community in learning about improving instruction with the Internet, helping students broadcast live from a studio and developing schoolwide technology policies with the principal.

Holt believes that if you give people — both children and adults — knowledge, materials and encouragement, and empower them to take leadership roles, they will meet the highest expectations. In building a community of leaders, Holt says her greatest reward is watching people grow personally and professionally.

So far, this approach has worked. For the third straight year at this school at which 90 percent of the students qualify for free- and reduced-priced lunch, more than 80 percent of the student population have passed the statewide assessment exam. Clearly, the school's energy and leadership translate into measurable student achievement gains.

Tie the daily operations of the schoolhouse to school and student learning goals

Everything a principal does sends a signal to the school community regarding what they personally value and what the school believes in. The appearance of the physical plant sends a signal. Whether or not student work is displayed on the walls sends a signal of what the principal and the school find important. One can get a sense of the values of a school within the first few minutes of walking in.

Principals will never get away from the administrative duties involved in running the school. Principals attend to the daily demands associated with the management of any organization. But these administrative duties are not disconnected from the core learning goals of the school. Creating the school budget, for instance, concretely aligns resources with instructional needs. Hiring decisions demonstrate whether the school community is dedicated to learning and growth. What may seem to be mundane administrative functions must be done with the school's vision in mind.

All school decisions should be based on the answer to one central question: How will this action improve the teaching and learning process?

Principals' Voices:

"Managers do things right; leaders do the right thing."

Legitimate Questions Followers Can Ask of Leaders

In *Leadership Jazz*, Max DePree writes that it is important that leaders think of their followers as volunteers. They don't have to stay in one place. They don't have to work for one company or for one leader. They follow someone only when she deserves it. Leaders and followers are all parts of a circle. Followers really determine how successful a leader will be.

Several questions leaders should expect from followers:
- What may I expect from you?
- Can I achieve my own goals by following you?
- Will I reach my potential by working with you?
- Can I entrust my future to you?
- Have you bothered to prepare yourself for leadership?
- Are you ready to be ruthlessly honest?
- Do you have the self-confidence and trust to let me do my job?
- What do you believe?

Source: DePree, Max. *Leadership Jazz*. New York: Dell Publishing. 1992.

Focus on Practice:

Wearing the Multiple Hats of the Principal
Daniels Farm School, Connecticut

Each day, the principal is faced with an unending list of tasks, decisions and responsibilities. But how does one balance the daily managerial issues of running the school with the need to serve as an instructional leader in the classroom?

In Trumbull, Connecticut, the elementary school principals are working together to define the managerial challenges in order to find the time for the instructional responsibilities. Gail Karwoski, principal of the Daniels Farm School, describes it as balancing the left side and the right side of the principalship.

As manager of this surburban school with more than 600 students, 94 percent of whom are white, Karwoski oversees everything from buses and lunches to parent involvement, recognizing that neglecting these issues can impede success in the classroom. But together with her colleagues across the district, Karwoski is making a concerted effort to stress "right" side of instructional efforts while delegating "left" responsibilities to emails, secretaries, lead teachers and others.

To include more teachers in instructional decision-making, Karwoski is forming instructional leadership teams. The idea is to empower and train teacher-leaders and also to provide more hands and minds to take on the management duties. A lead teacher provides managerial support before and after school. This allows Karwoski to focus on instructional issues, such as special education and supporting new classroom teachers.

"We all know that principals need to be committed and strong instructional leaders to effect sustained growth and improvement in our schools," Karwoski said. "But we must strike balance between our leadership responsibilities and our management duties. Neglecting one for the other can seriously impede student and school success."

"It begins with the natural feeling that one wants to serve, to serve first. Then, conscious choice brings one to aspire to lead. The difference manifests itself in the care taken by the servant — first to make sure the other people's highest needs are being served. The best test is: Do those served grow as persons; do they, while being served, become healthier, wiser, freer, more autonomous, more likely themselves to become servants?"

Robert Greenleaf
(1977)

Questions for Further Reflection

There is little doubt that the job of today's principal is more complex than it has ever been. Among the managerial tasks, the instructional challenges of leading the academic achievement of the school and the personal development of student, teacher and principal alike, the successful principal bears multiple responsibilities.

To balance the leadership and management responsibilities today's principal faces, one must:

• Create and foster a community of learners
How do the adults in this school take responsibility for their own learning and for that of their colleagues? How do we know that adults in the school are engaged as active learners? How do I, as principal, encourage and support this learning?

• Embody learner-centered leadership
What does learner-centered leading mean to me? What would it look like if it were truly happening in this school? How am I showing others in the school that I, too, am a learner and a teacher?

• Seek leadership contributions from multiple sources
How are teachers and others involved in making decisions that affect the school and student achievement? Who in the school believes that they have authority to make decisions? How are the skills and knowledge of different players in the school made public?

• Tie the daily operations of the schoolhouse to school and
  student learning goals
Over what and how much authority does the principal have in order to dramatically improve student achievement? Over what and how will teachers be held accountable for student results? Do personnel decisions reflect continual learning and growth in the school? Does the school budget represent the school's vision, values, and priorities? Do school policies reinforce an old model of authority? Do we use practices that make learning and growing safe for adults but risky for children?

Standard One Strategies

Use the Questions for Further Reflection to help you think about and rate the degree to which each Standards One strategy is evident in your school or your practice as a school leader.

1 – Not evident in my school/practice
2 – Somewhat or occasionally evident in school/practice
3 – Consistently evident in school/practice
4 – Consistently evident, with practices that elaborate upon or exceed expectation

Self-Assessment: Beginning of the Year

	1	2	3	4
Create and foster a community of learners				
Embody learner-centered leadership				
Seek leadership contributions from multiple sources				
Tie the daily operations of the schoolhouse to school and student learning goals				

Self-Assessment: Middle of the Year

	1	2	3	4
Create and foster a community of learners				
Embody learner-centered leadership				
Seek leadership contributions from multiple sources				
Tie the daily operations of the schoolhouse to school and student learning goals				

Self-Assessment: End of the Year

	1	2	3	4
Create and foster a community of learners				
Embody learner-centered leadership				
Seek leadership contributions from multiple sources				
Tie the daily operations of the schoolhouse to school and student learning goals				

For More Information

Resources From NAESP:

Educational Research Service, National Association of Elementary School Principals, and National Association of Secondary School Principals. *The Principal, Keystone of a High-Achieving School: Attracting and Keeping the Leaders We Need* (2000).

Doud J., and E. Keller. *A Ten-Year Study: The K-8 Principal in 1998* (1998).

On the Web:

Leadership for Learning from the North Central Regional Educational Laboratory (www.ncrel.org/cscd) features back issues of the publication, *New Leaders for Tomorrow's Schools, the Urban Learners Leadership Initiative*, focused on closing the achievement gap and family involvement surveys.

Association of Supervision and Curriculum Development (www.ascd.org) has numerous books, articles and videos available online as well as searchable back issues of ASCD's monthly publication, *Educational Leadership*.

From the Research:

Barth, R. *Improving School From Within: Teachers, Parents and Principals Can Make a Difference.* San Francisco: Jossey-Bass, 1990.

Fullan, M. *What's Worth Fighting For in the Principalship?* New York: Teachers College Press, 1997.

Greenleaf, R. *Servant-Leadership: A Journey Into the Nature of Legitimate Power and Greatness.* New York: Paulist Press, 1977.

Leithwood, K., D. Jantzi, and R. Steinbach. *Changing Leadership for Changing Times.* Buckingham, UK: Open University Press, 1999.

Sergiovanni, T. *Leadership for the Schoolhouse: How Is It Different? Why Is It Important?* San Francisco: Jossey-Bass, 1996.

Standard Two: Set High Expectations and Standards

Effective principles set high expectations and standards for the academic and social development of all students and the performance of adults.

I f we are serious about helping all students achieve at high levels, then principals must rethink the what, how and why of schooling, organized around high expectations and high standards. And they must be given the authority to hold people accountable for results. All policies, planning and decisions must be based on the belief that every child — quite apart from the accident of whether they were born in a low-income family, as a racial or language minority or with a physical or learning disability — can and will achieve at high levels.

This fundamental belief is the driving focus of a school community committed to continuous learning and improvement. What would it look like if school communities were to act on the belief that all students could achieve at high levels? We would see principals who:

- **Articulate a clear vision that reflects the beliefs, values and commitments of the school community**

- **Ensure that all students have adequate and appropriate opportunities to meet high standards**

- **Develop a school culture that is flexible, collaborative, innovative and supportive of efforts to improve achievement of all students**

Principals' Voices:

"What the principal does and says permeates the school building."

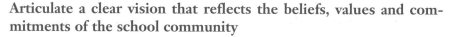

Articulate a clear vision that reflects the beliefs, values and commitments of the school community

There is considerable debate about how, exactly, a vision is created. Some people say the principal should establish a vision and then work to get other members of the school community to support it. Others say that true support will come only if members of the school community participate in creating a vision for the school and for students.

Visions should help others understand what the people in a school believe and are committed to. Furthermore, principals can and should make clear statements about what they, as school leaders, believe, which will set a direction for the beliefs the school community articulates.

A clear vision enables principals to come back to the fundamental beliefs that drive the actions of a school. This is an essential concept: If people in the school do not believe that all children are capable of learning at high levels, then some children will continue to fall through the cracks. If all of the people in the school don't see it as their responsibility to move children to higher levels of performance, then it simply won't occur.

These beliefs should encourage principals to ask essential questions and to implement non-traditional, "out-of-the-box" answers.

Principals' Voices:

"There should be evidence everywhere in the school of what you believe as a principal and what the school stands for."

Results of Shared Vision

Developing a clear vision shared by the entire school community can have a significant impact. Principals find that shared vision:

- Motivates and energizes people

- Creates a proactive orientation

- Gives direction to people within the organization

- Establishes specific standards of excellence

- Creates a clear agenda for action

Source: DuFour, R., and R. Eaker. *Professional Learning Communities at Work: Best Practices for Enhancing Student Achievement.* Bloomington, IN: National Educational Service, 1998.

Focus on Practice:
Finding More Hours in the School Day
Gladys Noon Spellman Elementary School, Maryland

With so many demands facing a principal and a school, it seems 26- or 30-hour days are needed. But can anything really be done to maximize time in the classroom and ensure that school hours are spent on instruction?

At Gladys Noon Spellman Elementary School in Cheverly, Maryland, school leaders have developed a time-management system that allows the large, multicultural elementary school in the Washington, D.C., suburbs to manage the disruptions and time issues that sidetrack similar schools.

Upon arriving at Spellman, Principal Sherry Liebs relied on her past experience at similar schools and set out to develop a block scheduling system that would allow the school to focus on improving literacy skills for its more than 750 students.

Based on the work of Robert Lynn Canady, the block scheduling structure implemented at Spellman provides teachers 90-minute segments of instructional time each morning for reading and language arts. In fact, before implementing the program, the school brought Canady in to talk with teachers about the opportunities available through block scheduling.

To further focus classroom time, each classroom teacher was provided a specialist, who served as an instructional partner. This teamwork allowed for small group instructional settings and provided teachers with experts who could make meaningful contributions to daily classroom lessons.

At Spellman, that one and one-half hour block each morning for reading instruction was designated untouchable. No announcements were made during that period. No assemblies or field trips were scheduled at that time. And the block would not be sacrificed for early dismissals or unexpected changes in the school day.

New Principal Ann Swann has continued this system, which is now used by all grades in the K-6 school. Also, it has allowed teachers to gain a greater focus of the school vision and provided an important instructional tool, even with 30 students in a classroom. And it has provided a new network of support and collaboration for the entire school staff. As one teacher put it, "It gave us the opportunity to teach. After all, that's why we're all here."

"Although not easy to define, mission and purpose instill the intangible forces that motivate teachers to teach, school leaders to lead, children to learn, and parents and the community to have confidence in their school."

Terrence Deal and Kent Peterson (1998)

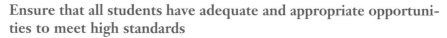

Ensure that all students have adequate and appropriate opportunities to meet high standards

High expectations and performance-driven schools mock the notion of equity if students, teachers and principals are not given a legitimate opportunity to meet standards.

The most fundamental opportunity-to-learn standards encompass the following areas:

- **Safety and school setting. Schools should be safe and conducive to learning.**

There is much we can do within school buildings to ensure a safe setting conducive to learning, such as providing engaging instruction, creating small learning communities where students and teachers know each other, teaching conflict resolution skills, providing accommodation rooms and providing clear standards for behavior and conduct. Support from the broader community is essential to accomplishing this.

- **Active and constructive learning environments. Schools should treat students as active learners who construct knowledge from meaningful experiences.**

Students are active, not passive, learners who learn best from tasks that require them to relate new facts, concepts and processes to their existing mental images and to their ongoing experiences. It is our collective responsibility to design settings that build on students' active learning capacity, multiple intelligences and amazing resiliency. It is our responsibility to monitor and implement intellectually rigorous curriculum that moves students toward higher levels of learning.

- **Developmentally appropriate. Schools should be socially and emotionally appropriate.**

Schools cannot be just about curriculum. A lot of learning deals with social and emotional factors of life that are not part of the academic content. One's self-concept is the basis of reality for individuals, determining what they perceive about themselves, which determines what actions they take — or don't. Children either believe they can or they can't.

Academic rigor and intellectual development must be combined with humanity. How children see themselves is largely influenced by how adults see and treat them. This outlook often determines whether students will try at all — or how much effort they'll make before they decide whether they can or can't. For instance, if a student believes she cannot write, evidence to support that judgment will seem to her to keep popping up. The determination children make about themselves makes the difference in whether students decide to revise a paper for a higher standard or only do the minimum expected. It determines who they hang out with, and whether they ask for extra help. It determines whether they participate in other school activities — whether they try out for the play or go out for sports. It is important for adults in the school to provide sufficiently varied activities so that all students can achieve success — both academically but also in social and personal aspects.

- **Time. Schedules, curricula, instructional strategies and assessments should give students the time they need to meet high academic standards.**

All students do not learn at the same pace. In the United States, most schools are open for a fixed 180 days per year, hold six hours of instruction per day, and deliver subject matter in 40-55 minute blocks of time. Within this narrow schedule, it is difficult for all students to achieve at high levels.

A successful formula would hold achievement as a constant but consider time to be a variable. Schools should have the resources to provide additional instructional time for the lowest-performing students. More flexible conceptions of time should be applied to professional staff so they may incorporate professional development and community building into their work schedules.

Principals' Voices:

"A high-quality staff must be on the 'same page' in terms of focus and commitment to enhancing student achievement in a safe and caring environment."

Focus on Practice:
Reinforcing the School Vision
Wilder Elementary School, North Dakota

If it's the beginning of the week, then it must be time for "Monday Morning Opening Live at Wilder Elementary School." For this Grand Forks elementary school, which has 153 students in preK through fifth grades, the school week begins with a school-wide assembly led by the principal.

At these gatherings, Principal Terry Brenner focuses the entire school on a "Habit of the Week," a process that allows all school learners to key in on one primary motivational lesson.

One week, for example, the school will commit: "I am responsible for my own learning." To practice this habit, Brenner will offer testimonials from students and provide practical examples of how teachers can put the lesson to practice. The result: a school with a shared vision of success in both deed and practice.

Through these regular gatherings, Brenner communicates a common sense of vision and direction. Together, they encourage and push one another to fulfill the week's goal and look forward to the lessons to be learned in the coming weeks.

One example is to open the school before the regular school day starts to support students who need extra help. Another example is to keep schools open and active between 3:00 p.m. and 6:00 p.m. Before- and after-school programs are critical for children of working families to connect with adults concerned for their welfare. And programs beyond the school day have been found to improve factors from children's attitudes about learning to attendance to homework completion

- **Resources. Schools should provide an equitable and adequate distribution of resources.**

Resource allocation decisions should rest with those closest to students. The community looks to the principal to use all available resources to ensure that the school is aligned to academic standards and that all students are learning at higher levels.

"Statements about vision incorporate the values and commitments that guide the system as well as beliefs about structure. These statements appeal to hearts as well as to minds; they command loyalty and emotional attachments and provide orientation for specific action."

Phillip Schlechty (1997)

Focus on Practice:
Building a Vision for All Children
Sunset Park Elementary School, North Carolina

A peaceful revolution took place at Sunset Park Elementary School in Wilmington, North Carolina, when Principal Deborah Parker took the helm. Stunned by low test scores and a low-performing school designation just months after starting as principal, Parker set about invigorating the school community with a solid vision, plan and goals toward success.

"All children, 100 percent, will achieve at or above grade level," declared Parker as she urged the school to adopt a new focus on literacy and character development. The plan to meet that vision included new programs, approaches and teaching strategies for this Title I school, at which 80 percent of the students qualify for free or reduced-price lunch.

Constantly preaching high expectations, Parker's mantra was to "up the ante." Again and again her students heard that they were the "best and the brightest." Parker issued more than 140 press releases explaining how Sunset Park was a model of school improvement. And parents were brought into the school regularly for workshops and parenting classes.

"By setting high expectations for the entire learning community," notes Parker, "and sharing a core set of values and beliefs, we have increased our overall proficiency from 40 percent to 85 percent in just four years." The school moved out of a low-performing status and met expected growth in academic success each year since 1997. Parker is clear on her purpose: "Being a principal requires a tenacious leader who is a keeper of the vision."

Develop a school culture that is flexible, collaborative, innovative and supportive of efforts to improve achievement of all students

Defined by a core set of beliefs, learning goals and sentiments, the school community comes together. Through this sense of common purpose and values, members of the learning community move from an individual sense of "I" to a collective sense of "we" in efforts to improve student performance.

In leading this community, the principal recognizes and appreciates the continual changes that affect it. Effective school leaders capitalize on the growing diversity of school populations and facilitate the contributions of each player. The principal also recognizes the challenges such a diversity in backgrounds and cultures poses in meeting the educational needs of all students, such as those coming from homes where English is not the primary language.

Effective school leaders ensure that the collaborative learning community understands the expectations and goals of the school and the school district. In addition, effective principals organize and focus the activities and decisions in the school to support key learning goals.

There is nothing routine about teaching and learning. Both require creativity, as well as know-how. If we are to succeed at having all children achieve at high levels, principals must insist that their school environments support continuous improvement. The best way to learn is to become actively involved in risky work. Open communication and sharing are the foundation for work that is collaborative and that requires risk. Joseph and Jo Blase write that principals support teacher development by:

- Providing time, space and money to implement ideas

- Reassuring people that ideas and plans, even when challenged, are valued

- Letting go through the growth process (not directing others, staying out of the way and allowing mistakes)

- Staying informed

- Providing open, friendly and supportive environments

To do so, principals need strong skills in providing open, constructive and accurate feedback and sensibility in creating the possibility of self-disclosure. Effective leaders know where they stand on particular issues and, at the same time, are committed to growth and change over time. Principals know that they do not have all the answers, but they are always thinking of new ways to build personal effectiveness and to help the people in their schools do the same. No one is free to avoid dealing with change or to stop the clocks to prepare for it, but a community of learners provides the principal and all those involved in the educational process with the tools and resources to manage and adapt to that change.

Principals' Voices:

"A school for me is centered around issues that are related to the achievement and development of children."

Questions for Further Reflection

The fundamental concept that all children can and will achieve at high levels is the driving focus of a school community committed to continuous learning and improvement. This belief creates an opportunity for principals to ask essential questions about the driving purpose behind their work in schools. Notable principals:

• Articulate a clear vision that reflects the beliefs, values and commitments of the school community

What is the vision I've articulated for my school? What underlying values and commitments underpin that vision? Have we clarified the beliefs that drive actions within this school? What evidence do I see that that statement has set a direction for others and influenced what is possible for children to accomplish?

• Ensure that all students have adequate and appropriate opportunities to meet high standards

What can we do to ensure that our students have fair opportunities to learn? How do we create safe learning environments for students? What active learning opportunities are available? What factors demonstrate that both our academic and non-academic programs are developmentally appropriate? How have we structured our time and resources to maximize learning?

• Develop a school culture that is flexible, collaborative, innovative and supportive of efforts to improve achievement of all students

What are the key learning goals on which we're focused? How are we articulating these to the community? What demonstrates, or hinders, our mutual respect? In what ways is my school a community? Do people feel a collective sense of "we" in our successes and challenges?

How am I innovative in my thinking? How do I help others be innovative? What makes our practice innovative and/or collaborative? How do I encourage creativity, imagination and risk-taking?

Standard Two Strategies

Use the Questions for Further Reflection to help you think about and rate the degree to which each Standards Two strategy is evident in your school or your practice as a school leader.

1 – Not evident in my school/practice

2 – Somewhat or occasionally evident in school/practice

3 – Consistently evident in school/practice

4 – Consistently evident, with practices that elaborate upon or exceed expectation

Self-Assessment: Beginning of the Year

	1	2	3	4
Articulate a clear vision that reflects the beliefs, values and commitments of the school community				
Ensure that all students have adequate and appropriate opportunities to meet high standards				
Develop a school culture that is flexible, collaborative, innovative and supportive of efforts to improve achievement of all students				

Self-Assessment: Middle of the Year

	1	2	3	4
Articulate a clear vision that reflects the beliefs, values and commitments of the school community				
Ensure that all students have adequate and appropriate opportunities to meet high standards				
Develop a school culture that is flexible, collaborative, innovative and supportive of efforts to improve achievement of all students				

Self-Assessment: End of the Year

	1	2	3	4
Articulate a clear vision that reflects the beliefs, values and commitments of the school community				
Ensure that all students have adequate and appropriate opportunities to meet high standards				
Develop a school culture that is flexible, collaborative, innovative and supportive of efforts to improve achievement of all students				

For More Information

On the Web:

Education World (www.education-world.com), a complete online resource for educators, features a school administrators' center (with a regular column and a rich archive of articles on leadership), "Wire Side Chats" with important names in education and extensive teacher-submitted lessons.

Children Achieving is Philadelphia's 10-point framework for comprehensive education reform. Among the 10 strategies, several outline supports for student learning (which are similar to opportunity-to-learn standards). (www.philsch.k12.pa.us/Children_Achieving/exec_summary.html)

From the Research:

Ackerman, R., G. Donaldson, Jr., and R. Van Der Bogert. *Making Sense As a School Leader: Persisting Questions, Creative Opportunities.* San Francisco: Jossey-Bass, 1996.

Blase, J. and J. Blase. *Empowering Teachers: What Successful Principals Do.* Thousand Oaks, CA: Corwin Press, 2000.

Deal, T. and K. Peterson. *Shaping School Culture: The Heart of Leadership.* San Francisco: Jossey-Bass, 1998.

Schlechty, P. *Inventing Better Schools: An Action Plan for Educational Reform.* San Francisco: Jossey-Bass, 1997.

Senge, P. *Schools That Learn: A Fifth Discipline Fieldbook for Educators, Parents and Everyone Who Cares About Education.* New York: Doubleday, 2000.

Standard Three: Demand Content and Instruction That Ensure Student Achievement

Effective principals demand content and instruction that ensure student achievement of agreed-upon academic standards.

Successful schools are organized around student learning. The ability of the principal to guide instructional improvement is key to creating standards-based change. Increasing pressure for student performance is pushing principals into bearing primary responsibility for school and instructional improvement. This role of instructional leadership in service to increased student learning is new to many principals.

Principals recognize that children learn at different paces, but they make sure that all children master key subjects and can read, write and calculate on or above grade level in preparation for moving on to higher levels of learning. Student effort is supported by rigorous content and instruction, which are continually assessed through multiple forms of assessment, regular observations and evaluation.

But as Elaine Fink of the San Diego City Schools says, "It's not just about content, it's about leadership. It's about the message you send by what you do, by the urgency you create, by the hard honest conversations you have with people and the hard decisions you make and by acknowledging what you're really seeing — and not sugar-coating it. You have to be able to inspire people if you want to lead. If they believe in you, they will go along with you."

Principals' Voices:

"Quality schools have a clearly defined set of academic standards and curriculum understood by teachers, students, parents and the community."

What would it look like if principals were providing leadership for high-quality instruction in schools and classrooms? We'd see principals who:

> • **Hire and retain high-quality teachers and hold them responsible for student learning**
>
> • **Monitor alignment of curriculum with standards, school goals and assessments**
>
> • **Observe classroom practices to assure that all students are meaningfully engaged in active learning**
>
> • **Provide up-to-date technology and instructional materials**
>
> • **Review and analyze student work to determine whether students are being taught to standard**

Hire and retain high-quality teachers and hold them responsible for student learning

Teacher expertise is arguably one of the most important factors in determining student achievement. And to be effective, teachers need to know both their subject matter and how to teach it to diverse learners. Good teaching does matter — a lot. A report from researcher Dr. William Sanders indicates that students who have several effective teachers in a row make dramatic gains in achievement, while those who have even two consecutive ineffective teachers lose significant ground that they may never recover. Indeed, students who achieve at similar levels in the third grade may be separated by as many as 50 percentile points three years later depending on the quality of the teachers to whom they were assigned. The differences are even more acute for poor children.

Effective principals do whatever is in their power to ensure that every classroom in the school has a certified, qualified teacher. Effective principals also work to retain teachers. They provide working conditions that support high-quality instruction, including streamlined recruitment and hiring efforts, reduced teacher load, access to appropriate teaching resources, facilities, time for adequate individual and common planning, moral support and opportunities for reflection.

Notable principals also provide regular evaluations that hold teachers responsible for student learning. Teachers are the key to improved instruction and student

Principals' Voices:

"It all comes together when school staff work together to meet the individual needs of all students, learning is integrated and connected, and the differing learning styles of students are addressed daily."

performance. But if schools are to be places where good teachers thrive and continual improvement of instruction occurs, it is strong principals who must demand that everyone rise to the same standard.

Effective instructional leaders evaluate teachers based on their instructional effectiveness as demonstrated by student achievement. Through these evaluations, principals document ineffective teachers and assist them in improving their teaching practice. One difficult issue for principals to address is when and how to dismiss ineffective teachers.

Focus on Practice:
Unique Use of Space for Two Instructional Paths in One School
Cherry Creek Elementary School, Indiana

Managing parents' ideas for a new instructional program was more an opportunity than a chore at Cherry Tree Elementary School in Carmel Clay, Indiana. Principal Don Setterlof led a group of parents and teachers in designing a 21st Century School model nearly a decade ago. Now, students have a choice between two distinct learning environments in the same building.

Overall, Cherry Tree has 640 students in kindergarten through fifth grade. In the traditional elementary school section of the building, children attend class with their peers. In the 21st Century School, students of multiple ages work together in a primary class (grades 1-3) and an intermediate class (grades 4-5).

The 21st Century School allows a flexible curriculum developed around four key themes each year, with each theme studied for nine full weeks. The curriculum is developed around state standards, and parents are provided regular updates through newsletters, focus groups and quarterly parent-teacher conferences.

Cherry Tree is successfully moving all of its students forward. Over 95 percent of students passed the statewide mathematics and language arts assessments. Setterlof says students in both schools are closely matched in terms of academic performance.

"Our challenge has been to keep the lines of communication open so that there are no misunderstandings among parents," Setterlof said. "We work hard to ensure that everyone understands our intent and what we are actually doing."

"A school leader? Quite simply, he or she is a person who can guide instructional improvement."

Richard Elmore
(1996)

Monitor alignment of curriculum with standards, school goals and assessments

Principals have to understand academic standards before they can get their school community to align curriculum to standards and to school goals. Principals aren't able to know everything that is taught in every classroom and every grade, but they need a firm grasp of the curriculum and the grade-level objectives for each subject. Principals must have a good understanding of the developmental stages of children and how to create an environment that is developmentally appropriate. They must know how to lead their teachers to effectively implement appropriate instructional strategies.

Curriculum-alignment processes help teachers understand the relationship between what they teach and how students perform on standardized tests. It is an important opportunity for teachers to talk about expectations, teaching and student work. In some schools, instructional specialists and teachers work together to create performance-based practice assessments. This gives teachers a deeper understanding of what instruction is needed for students to perform well on assessments.

Principals' Voices:

"Teachers need the resources to make good instructional decisions, within a solid framework determined by the school community. This year, more than half of our classroom teachers are non-tenured. They need my attention. Our discussions and interactions are vital to their professional development."

Skills of Instructional Leaders

According to the *American School Board Journal*, strong instructional leaders are highly skilled in four areas:

1. They're well-informed about curriculum and instruction, and especially knowledgeable about teaching methods that emphasize having students solve problems and construct knowledge.

2. They know cognitive learning theories that help all students, especially low achievers, become competent learners.

3. They're adept at evaluating instruction, including giving teachers useful feedback so they can teach better and students can learn more.

4. They're able to set and maintain learning standards, including describing good teaching and good student work.

Source: Black, S. "Finding Time To Lead." *American School Board Journal.*
September 2000.

Observe classroom practices to assure that all students are meaningfully engaged in active learning

Effective principals spend large amounts of time in classrooms, observing the teaching of academic units and provide detailed feedback regarding how teachers' effectiveness can be improved. The point of principal and peer observations is not to catch a teacher doing something wrong. The point is to ensure that all students are meaningfully engaged, actively learning, and that teachers are not simply presenting material.

An important part of classroom observations is to evaluate the instructional skills of individual teachers, to assist these teachers in improving those skills and to help them grow professionally. Collaboration with other teachers and assignment of a mentor may be strategies a principal suggests to assist the teacher, but the conversation often begins between principal and teacher.

School leaders support teachers' professionalism by sharing feedback with teachers about objectives of lessons, the degree of student engagement and the behavior of students.

For new principals in particular, it is essential to be active and involved in the classroom as a dependable presence in the student learning process. Through such involvement, the principal can help teachers instill a sense of success for all students — a feeling that is vastly important to improved student performance.

Principals and lead teachers look to see whether teachers are teaching the academic units. They assess scope and sequence of the lesson. They look at whether the lesson fits generally with the larger curriculum concepts for the course of the year. They ask whether the assignments teachers are giving students are tied to standards. They look at the work students are doing to determine whether students are actively engaged in the concept of the lesson.

Effective principals review student work, post student work and talk with students about what they are learning. Because an effective principal is often in the classroom, students get to know that the principal is concerned about their learning. The message is that each student is responsible for his or her own learning.

Principals' Voices:

"Good instructional leaders seize every opportunity presented to them in their daily conversations with teachers, students and parents to convert 'casual conversation' about kids or what is happening in a classroom into an 'instructional conversation' in which they use inquiry. They find ways to change the conversation so that learning may occur."

Provide up-to-date technology and instructional materials

Just as it has in other sectors of society, technology can fundamentally transform how schools and teachers serve students. Technology can connect teachers and students to enormously expanded educational resources and individualized instruction. And it can expand the boundaries of the education setting beyond the classroom.

Technology can also profoundly improve the administrative procedures that support classroom instruction, helping to report development, inventory control, scheduling and hosts of other administrative matters. Principals and other school leaders make sure that teachers have adequate resources and professional development to use technology as an integral part of daily instruction.

Teachers naturally see the school's investment in their endeavor as a tangible indicator of support. As a result, teachers respond with a greater willingness to support school initiatives. Perhaps when teachers perceive that they have been given what they deem necessary to teach well, they are more willing to exert maximum effort. Whatever the reason, this support is extremely important to teachers and is an important part of the success of schools.

Developing Curriculum

There are five assumptions one might consider when guiding a curriculum development process:

1. Teachers should work collaboratively to design research-based curriculum that reflects the best thinking in each subject area.

2. The curriculum should help teachers, students, and parents clarify the specific knowledge, skills, and dispositions that students should acquire as a result of their schooling.

3. The results-oriented curriculum should reduce content and enable all parties to focus on essential and significant learning.

4. The curriculum process should enable an individual teacher, a teaching team, and the school to monitor student achievement at the classroom level.

5. Curriculum and assessment processes should foster commitment to continuous improvement.

Source: DuFour, R., and R. Eaker. *Professional Learning Communities at Work: Best Practices for Enhancing Student Achievement.* Bloomington, IN: National Educational Service, 1998.

Focus on Practice:

Walking Through and Talking About Instruction
Sterling B. Martin Middle School, Texas

"What are your expectations in this classroom? How will I know if your students are learning?" asks Principal Rheba Jones as she talks to a teacher at Sterling B. Martin Middle School in Corpus Christi, Texas.

Jones leads a team of observers into every classroom of this 700-student school. As a group, they establish their purpose for visiting. They observe the student work on the walls, current assignments, cumulative portfolios and journals. Then, they debrief as a group, asking such questions as "What did we see today? Where are we moving as a school? Did you see evidence of progress in this classroom? Are we moving quickly enough?"

It is all part of a walkthrough process based on inquiry developed by the Learning Research and Development Center at the University of Pittsburgh. "This process moved our school from defining clear expectations to academic rigor," said Jones.

This urban middle school, which is 98 percent Latino and at which 78 percent of the students qualify for free or reduced-price lunch, has made significant progress. Just three years ago, the school barely held off the state's low-performing designation. The school is now considered "exemplary," with 80 percent of the students mastering statewide assessments.

In addition to an ongoing focus on literacy, this year the school is also focused on accountable talk. Students are expected to talk about their learning and demonstrate their understanding. Staff members are expected to focus all of their discussion on how learning happens and how it could be better.

Jones sees progress: "When we started this work we knew it needed to happen, but it was much bigger than we ever thought. We're moving forward now."

Principals' Voices:

"If you don't have the expertise to improve instruction in a specific area, you have to manage time and resources to build that critical knowledge."

Focus on Practice:
Students Can Do No Better Than the Assignments They Are Given
Lincoln Elementary School, Florida

For academic standards to be achieved, they must be incorporated into the day-to-day activities of all those who educate students. By applying them every day, instead of just after tests have been taken, a school can truly ensure that all students succeed.

At Lincoln Elementary School in West Palm Beach, Florida, that is exactly what has been done. Rather than accept excuses and lowered expectations, this K-6 school with 1070 students adopted an aggressive strategy for educating and training teachers in the standards by which they would be measured.

Principal Francina Bain turned to the Education Trust's Standards in Practice (SIP) program to provide her teachers with the tools and knowledge needed to have a positive impact in the classroom. Working with SIP trainers, she built a professional development program for Lincoln teachers that focused on state standards, how to teach to them and how to properly assess student work.

"We taught the standards, not the test," Bain said. "It was a lot of work, but well worth it. Now, all our teachers know the standards, where their students are and where they need to be moved."

Lincoln Elementary School's standards-based approach to learning was not limited to organized professional development programs. Every week, school-day planning time and after-school meetings guide progress. Standards are discussed at every staff meeting. Parents, too, have been included in the process and are provided both and understanding of school standards and the tools to aid in student learning at home.

For the students, this approach has already reaped benefits. On recent tests, Lincoln students increased their reading skills performance 21 percent, their writing skills performance 35 percent and their math skills performance 19 percent.

1 Leadership | **2** Vision | **3** Student Learning | **4** Adult Learning | **5** Data & Decision-Making | **6** Community Engagement

37

Review and analyze student work to determine whether students are being taught to standard

Principals and others who lead instruction do not leave student performance to chance. They provide the resources and support necessary at every juncture to improve the content of what is taught and the method by which it is taught. And they periodically review students' work to ensure that it is aligned with standards.

Specifically, school leaders can help teachers use student work as an important piece of information about the rigor of their assignments, whether the assignment is aligned to the level of the academic standards taught and whether students are achieving what is expected of them.

Students in effective schools perform well on assessments because they are taught what the district or state expected them to learn. Leaders in these schools ensure — along the way, not just at the testing endpoint — that children are being taught the knowledge, concepts and skills articulated in state or district standards and measured in authentic assessments.

Technology Standards for School Success

Technology is a critical tool in improving teaching and learning. Using technology effectively is the challenge for every principal. The Collaborative for Technology Standards for School Administrators (TSSA Collaborative) has developed Technology Standards for School Administrators to help in this task.

The technology standards and objectives allow school principals to measure their success using technology. They may be helpful to principals as they bolster in-service professional development programs, school accountability and student assessments.

For more information on the Technology Standards for School Administrators, visit http://cnets.iste.org/tssa/

Questions for Further Reflection

Quality teachers, aligned curriculum, constructive feedback on classroom practice and up-to-date technology are critical components of effective instruction. Principals can gauge their schools' support for rigorous instruction with the following questions:

- Hire and retain high-quality teachers and hold them responsible for student learning

In what ways do I convey the utmost important of quality teaching and teachers? How do I recognize and support quality teachers? What hiring practices can I use to increase the number of effective teachers in on the faculty? What do I do to help ineffective teachers and remove those who will not/cannot improve?

- Monitor alignment of curriculum with standards, school goals and assessments

What opportunities do I use to learn what I need to about the curriculum and grade-level objectives about each subject? What opportunities do teachers in my building have to participate in curriculum alignment processes? How do teachers use those opportunities to talk about expectations, teaching and student work?

- Observe classroom practices to assure that all students are meaningfully engaged in active learning

How often am I in classrooms? What shows me evidence of good teaching and high levels of learning? What kinds of feedback do I share with teachers after observing their classes? Does this feedback focus on the teacher's lessons, methods of instruction and student learning? Does it focus on the extent to which all students were engaged in meaningful/relevant instructional activities? How do I use what I learn from students and student work/performance to help teachers improve their practices?

- Provide up-to-date technology and instructional materials

How do we use technology and other resources to support instruction? Do members of my school community have the technology they need to do the best job possible? Do they have the training they need to take full advantage of technology?

- Review and analyze student work to determine whether students are being taught to standard

Do I offer the necessary resources to allow students to learn and grasp curriculum aligned with standards? Do I periodically review students' work to ensure that it is meeting a high standard? Are teachers adequately trained and supported to look at student work to determine the rigor of assignments and their alignment with standards?

Standard Three Strategies

Use the Questions for Further Reflection to help you think about and rate the degree to which each Standard Three strategy is evident in your school or your practice as a school leader.

1 – Not evident in my school/practice

2 – Somewhat or occasionally evident in school/practice

3 – Consistently evident in school/practice

4 – Consistently evident, with practices that elaborate upon or exceed expectation

Self-Assessment: Beginning of the Year

	1	2	3	4
Hire and retain high-quality teachers and hold them responsible for student learning				
Monitor alignment of curriculum with standards, school goals and assessments				
Observe classroom practices to assure that all students are meaningfully engaged in active learning				
Provide up-to-date technology and instructional materials				
Review and analyze student work to determine whether students are being taught to standard				

Self-Assessment: Middle of the Year

	1	2	3	4
Hire and retain high-quality teachers and hold them responsible for student learning				
Monitor alignment of curriculum with standards, school goals and assessments				
Observe classroom practices to assure that all students are meaningfully engaged in active learning				
Provide up-to-date technology and instructional materials				
Review and analyze student work to determine whether students are being taught to standard				

Self-Assessment: End of the Year

	1	2	3	4
Hire and retain high-quality teachers and hold them responsible for student learning				
Monitor alignment of curriculum with standards, school goals and assessments				
Observe classroom practices to assure that all students are meaningfully engaged in active learning				
Provide up-to-date technology and instructional materials				
Review and analyze student work to determine whether students are being taught to standard				

For More Information

Resources From NAESP:

Essentials for Principals: School Leader's Guide to Special Education (2001).

On the Web:

The Mid-continent Regional Educational Laboratory (McREL) (www.mcrel.org) contains rich instructional resources, including:

- A database of standards and benchmarks and aligned activities (www.mcrel.org/standards-benchmarks)
- Research into Practice modules with a step-by-step guide for engaging school staff in an examination of critical research and its implications for the classroom (www.mcrel.org/resources/services/rips.asp)

FREE (www.ed.gov/free), from the U.S. Department of Education, links educators to hundreds of federally supported teaching and learning resources. The site links to the Gateway to Educational Materials (www.thegateway.org), a database of more than 17,000 education resources across more than 100 Web sites.

MiddleWeb (www.middleweb.org), a Web site full of resources for middle school teachers, principals, parents and schools, features current news stories; lesson plans, teaching strategies and ideas about classroom management; and insights into assessment, standards-driven teachers and integrated curriculum.

From the Research:

Barkley, S., et. al. "Leadership Matters: Building Leadership Capacity." Atlanta: Southern Regional Education Board, April 2001.

DuFour, R. and R. Eaker. *Professional Learning Communities at Work: Best Practices for Enhancing Student Achievement.* Bloomington, IN: National Educational Service, 1998.

Sanders, W. and Rivers, J. "Cumulative Residual Effects of Teachers on Future Student Academic Achievement." 1998.

Standard Four: Create a Culture of Adult Learning

Effective principals create a culture of continuous learning for adults tied to student learning and other school goals.

Research shows that what teachers know about the subjects they teach and whether they have access to the latest research and materials on those subjects is essential to achieving high levels of student performance. Indeed, one study shows that every additional dollar spent on more highly qualified teachers produces greater increases in student achievement than dollars spent on things other than instruction.

The value of professional development once was measured by how many teachers attended an event and whether they indicated on a mimeographed page that they enjoyed it. Criteria for effective professional development have become more rigorous. Today, professional development activities are considered effective if they lead to changes in practice of adults and the performance of students

Simply providing more opportunities for professional development isn't enough. It's the quality of what's offered that counts. Professional development must be more focused on high-quality instruction and student work. It must happen in real time, in school and be more team-based. It must be pegged to improved student learning.

Principals are key to providing the support and learning opportunities teachers and staff need to improve instruction and boost student achievement. Principals recognize that staff members are learners, just as they are teachers, and must have the instructional and development tools they need to pursue their own learning and growth.

An effective principal works to provide every teacher and staff member with the tools to learn and improve professionally. Development opportunities are not just for teachers, however, and principals, leading by example, should identify professional development opportunities to improve their own craft.

Principals' Voices:

"I believe that principals are in the human development business. We facilitate the learning of children, teachers and other adults associated with our schools."

What would it look like if principals were successfully providing the culture and climate for continued adult learning and development in the school? We would see principals who:

- **Provide time for reflection as an important part of improving practice**

- **Invest in teacher learning**

- **Connect professional development to school learning goals**

- **Provide opportunities for teachers to work, plan and think together**

- **Recognize the need to continually improve principals' own professional practice**

Provide time for reflection as an important part of improving practice

Effective instructional leaders recognize that reflection is an important part of continuous improvement. They also recognize that reflection is not a one-time exercise; they use the process as a tool for ongoing assessments of the progress of attitude shifts, behavioral changes and differences in practice. By making time for reflection, principals and teachers alike demonstrate their belief in the responsibility for their own learning. Taking the time to reflect provides an opportunity to evaluate our past actions and build stronger future activities and teaching situations.

Invest in teacher learning

Learning and development are career-long ambitions for teachers and principals. And principals who demonstrate support for adult learning in the school create opportunities for professional learning in the daily schedule of teachers. In its standards for professional development, the National Staff Development Council (NSDC) advocates that at least 25 percent of teachers' time be devoted to their own learning and to collaboration with colleagues.

In addition to protecting time in the school day, the commitment of instructional leaders shows up in the school budget, with a percentage (ideally, 5 to 10 percent, NSDC says) of funding going to the professional development opportunities for teachers and other instructional staff.

Effective instructional leaders understand how to identify and meet the development needs of all the individuals who work in the school building. Through this understanding, the principal works to build a staff development program that reflects on overall school improvement — focusing on the development of both the students and the adults in the school.

A detailed and responsive professional development calendar provides the time and opportunity for adult learners to apply new ideas in the classroom. Meaningful professional development nurtures the growth of all individuals in the school community, and a successful principal ensures that lessons learned as part of a staff development program are regularly shared with all members of the school community.

At the same time, the principal will engage in one-on-one discussions with faculty and staff, identifying classroom concerns and successes. By identifying individual professional development plans for teachers, the principal provides needed leadership in instruction, while providing the individualized support and attention that produces similarly attentive and concerned teachers.

Successful staff development is executed in a school environment that encourages the development and expression of individual capabilities and emphasizes the worth of the individual, as well as the community.

Principals' Voices:

"Our profession is a people profession. If a principal doesn't put people first he/she misses the full essence of the job."

Connect professional development to school learning goals

Expectations determine results — not just for students but for adults. Schools leaders committed to improvement and growth establish goals for this. Professional development must be tied to learning goals of the school.

Principals should periodically review the learning goals of the school. In addition, the principal should determine which students have not met the learning goals. This information can then help determine what professional development is needed to improve instruction for those students. Professional development needs are assessed on a variety of measures, including observations and evaluations of classroom performance and instructional practices; one-on-one conversations with teachers; or small-group discussions with grade-level or subject-area teams that focus on student work, test scores, portfolios, performance-based exams or other measures of student learning.

The success of professional development activities should be based not only on whether teacher practice changes, but on whether student performance increases. Student learning is indicated by improved scores on norm-referenced tests, performance assessments, district- and teacher-constructed assessments and success in advanced-level courses. Student results are measured specifically in terms of academic achievement, rather than nonacademic measures such as classroom behaviors or attitudes.

Focus on Practice:
Shared Culture
Briar Glen School, Illinois

"We're going to make it together," preaches Briar Glen School Principal Joan Vydra. Working with teachers and parents, she also practices it, building a school organization focused on students and academic achievement.

When she first arrived at this K-5 school with 500 students (74 percent white; 12 percent Asian-Pacific Islander; 9 percent African-American) in the Chicago suburb of Wheaton. Vydra recognized that the faculty spent much of its time on organizational issues, managing each classroom individually at the expense of leading instructionally. Classes were run just fine, but where was the school headed?

A veteran principal, Vydra refocused teachers on instructional issues, moving all staff members forward through a comprehensive school improvement plan. She helped teachers by serving as a conduit for data collection and interpretation, and sought out funds to pay teachers to develop standards-based newsletters for the community.

Her efforts went beyond the schoolhouse doors. Vydra worked with parents to identify school events that were of the greatest importance to parents. She made sure that teachers were present for those events, cultivating communication and a sense of respect between teachers and parents.

Briar Glen School's success is the result of a team effort. Together, the principal, the teachers, the parents and the students have built a shared culture of learning, a culture rooted in communication, teamwork and student achievement.

Provide opportunities for teachers to work, plan and think together

Isolation is the enemy of learning. Principals who support the learning of adults in their school organize teachers' schedules to provide opportunities for teachers to work, plan and think together. For instance, teams of teachers who share responsibility for the learning of all students meet regularly to plan lessons, critique student work and the assignments that led to it and solve common instructional or classroom management problems.

Effective professional development allows teachers to learn from and teach their fellow faculty members, through continued discussions, demonstrations and assistance. This team approach allows the school to grow and develop as a single unit, providing the natural development of teacher leaders, coaches, mentors and supporters. By closely tying professional development to the school learning goals, the principal encourages all staff to make meaningful contributions to classroom performance, enabling them to serve as active leaders and learners within the schoolhouse.

Many schools create blocks of instructional time during which teachers meet and plan together. In some schools, staff come together twice a week to share experiences and strategies that achieve positive results.

Principals' Voices:

"The only power any of us has is the ability to change the conversation. This is truly the essence of instructional leadership."

National Staff Development Council Standards for Staff Development

The National Staff Development Council's revised Standards for Staff Development provide direction for designing a professional development experience that ensures educators acquire the necessary knowledge and skills. Staff development must be results-driven, standards-based and job-embedded.

The standards include context standards that emphasize learning communities, leadership and resources to support adult learning. There are process standards that explore use of data, evaluation, research, design, learning and collaboration in schools. And there are content standards that focus on equity, quality teaching and family involvement.

For more information, visit the Web page at www.nsdc.org.

Teachers should be encouraged to communicate the lessons they learn as part of a professional development program and to share their observations with their colleagues. They should be provided opportunities to visit with and observe other teachers in the classroom, both within their own school and in other schools in the district. Such observation allows teachers to learn from and share with other educators.

Common planning time. Principals set expectations that teachers will continually seek information about academic content and instruction. Teachers often learn as much from each other as they do from outside sources. Their planning efforts are central to the improvement of instruction in schools.

Focus on Practice:
Principals Supporting Principals
Chula Vista, California

Chula Vista is the largest K-6 district in California, with more than 23,000 students. Just miles from the Mexico border, principals and staff face a wide variety of challenges helping students overcome language, social, cultural and health barriers to learning. Like anywhere else in United States, the most precious commodity for principals is time.

At the urging of Superintendent Libia Gil, principals are working together in new ways across the district. It wasn't easy, but in the 1990s, a task force of principals designed a rubric-based performance standard aligned with ISLLC standards. Now, principals are evaluated by both the superintendent and a group of peers, who observe classrooms, analyze student work and conduct formal interviews with key staff and parent leaders.

The principals are expected to perform according to standards describing instructional strategies, staff supervision, hiring and leadership, building communities with parents and students, building culture and other measures. Bonuses are tied to the results.

Principals are grouped in peer groups of four to seven members who work together to provide support and feedback to each other. According to Gil, this includes "classroom observations, analysis of student work, formal interviews with key staff and parent leaders, as well as problem-solving and idea exchanges on best practices."

The district has recently developed a Leadership Learning Institute, in an attempt to stretch leadership capacity and develop the mechanisms for lifelong, collaborative learning efforts.

---

1 Leadership | **2** Vision | **3** Student Learning | **4** Adult Learning | **5** Data & Decision-Making | **6** Community Engagement

47

Focus on Practice:
Building a Culture Around the Special Needs of Students
O'Hearn Elementary School, Massachusetts

Inclusion is a daunting challenge. Integrating general education and special education students can pose resource, instructional and training issues for the school and the district and can be a political lightning rod for the community.

Every child can succeed is the heart of the school culture at O'Hearn Elementary School in Boston, Massachusetts. Principal Bill Henderson, who himself is visually impaired, made a commitment to provide the best possible education to every child, regardless of physical or developmental limitations. But how could Henderson ensure that students with Down Syndrome, autism and cerebral palsy receive the equal education in regular classrooms mandated by federal and state law?

Early on, Henderson recognized that success required a team effort and a team commitment. He worked closely with the superintendent and the Boston School Committee. And parents, teachers and community leaders formed a task force to focus on school needs during the planning stages.

Today, the school has adopted a school-based management approach, as parents work with administrators and teachers on budget, personnel and instructional decisions. Teachers have also seized the mantle of leadership, developing the strategies and materials for implementing inclusion in general education classes. They have also taken personal responsibility for the professional development of new and veteran teachers and staff on the skills and knowledge-base needed to succeed at O'Hearn, where nearly 25 percent of the school's 213 K-5 students have some form of disability.

At O'Hearn, inclusion has yielded success. The school is one of Boston's higher performing schools and has consistently scored above the national average on standardized tests. Student attendance is usually at 95 percent and discipline problems are nearly nonexistent. O'Hearn is a place where a strong school culture has truly made a difference for every child.

Principals' Voices:

"A principal needs to ensure a strong and ongoing staff development program that increases teachers' capacity to use appropriate and varied instructional strategies based on who and what they are teaching."

"It's not just about content, its about leadership. It's about the message you send by what you do; the urgency you create; by the hard honest conversation you have with people and the hard decisions you make; and by acknowledging what you're really seeing."

Elaine Fink
(2001)

School leaders sometimes set aside space and time for teachers to plan and work together. Most of the time, planning time is focused on important instructional issues. Teachers carefully review students' work in comparison with academic standards and discuss opportunities for improving instruction. Time is used to create practice performance assessments, score the assessments and identify common areas of strength and need.

Planning times become important opportunities for teachers to learn from and share with each other. They are also times for teachers to pursue their individual professional development plans. Planning time allows a principal or lead teacher to bring teachers together from different disciplines to talk about interdisciplinary planning and effective teaching strategies. Planning time helps teachers prioritize skills, concepts and content.

Focus on Practice:

Supporting Aspiring and Experienced School Leaders in San Diego
San Diego City Schools, California

San Diego's Educational Leadership Development Academy, a collaborative project of the school district, local universities and other education agencies, provides a unique continuum of support and training to new and experienced school leaders.

Programs within the continuum are designed to identify and develop teachers with leadership potential, assist new principals and enable experienced principals to deepen their knowledge and skill levels. All of the Academy's leadership training is job-embedded; it links learning to the immediate and real-life problems faced by school administrators through training programs followed by coaching.

Among the programs for new and experienced principals are monthly instructional conferences for all principals, full-time mentor principals and up to 25 coaching principals.

Eight district-level instructional leaders support these mentor and coaching principals and work directly with school principals. They conduct regular instructional visits to schools, discussing research, expert teaching practices, the school's progress and the principal's instructional skills and knowledge.

All of the Academy's programs are focused on developing principals who will provide leadership, direction and vision for schools as learning communities.

Subject-area or grade-level meetings. Learning opportunities should include both principals and other instructional leaders. In grade-level or subject-area teams, principals and teachers work together to review student work — and the assignments that lead to it. In addition, working with teachers enables principals an opportunity to develop professional development plans tied to individual needs.

Principals are key participants in professional development, and effective principals see themselves as team leaders and team members. Meetings with grade-level or subject-area teams allow a principal to create smaller learning communities in which teachers can encourage each other as learners. Within these smaller learning communities, principals are able to focus conversations on student work and the barriers to increasing student achievement. Looking at student work allows teachers to examine what they are assigning students and assessing what students are learning. Conversations about what teachers want students to learn can help to change instructional strategies to ensure that students are indeed learning it. Small group meetings are also an excellent way to share effective practices.

Coaching/mentoring. Instructional leaders recognize that, while they play a significant role in providing professional development, they are not the sole source. In addition to community contributions, professional development depends on teacher study groups, team activities and action research, all of which place teachers much more in charge of their own learning.

A valuable tool in this pursuit is coaching. By enlisting the help of expert teachers in the school, the principal can provide new teachers and teachers in need with a guide through the process. These coaches provide leadership in standards, content, instruction and other such issues, providing the foundations of quality teaching from those who have achieved it. Working both one-on-one and in teams, these coaches promote a sense of unity between teachers, providing site-based peer leadership in teacher development.

Collaboration at Toth Elementary School

Every month groups of teachers meet to reflect at Toth Elementary in Perrysburg, Ohio. Led by principal Beth Christoff, they ask themselves:

- Do we make decisions based upon the best knowledge available to us?

- Do we remain in agreement that we are committed to the belief that all of our students can learn?

- Do we have desired outcomes that are simple for all to understand, yet powerful for all of our students and staff?

- Do we believe that what we are doing remains important?

- Are decisions being made always in the best interest of our students?

The principal also serves a conduit of information, providing access to the wide range of opportunities and programs available to better teacher performance. For example, the successful principal encourages qualified, experienced teachers to pursue National Board certification. Principals also use and develop their networks to bring quality presenters and speakers to the school. They build relationships with local colleges and universities for continuing education opportunities, including facilitating participation in summer or evening training or skill acquisition and development programs.

A successful principal, no matter how new or senior in the field, also appreciates the value of and need for mentoring within the principal profession. The principal learns valuable lessons from other leaders. Just as a principal should institute a mentoring program for teachers within the school, today's principal should also view principal mentoring as a valuable tool resulting in improved leadership skills and, ultimately, a stronger learning environment.

ISLLC: Creating Standards and Standards-Based Professional Development for School Leaders

The Interstate School Leaders Licensure Commission's (ISLLC) Standards for School Leaders represent the collective wisdom of colleagues in schools, districts, universities and professional associations at both the state and national levels in defining the importance and the responsibilities of effective school leadership in 21st century schools.

In brief, the ISLLC standards call on school leaders to develop and articulate a vision of learning, advocate and sustain a school culture conducive to student learning and staff growth, ensure the management of a safe and effective learning environment, collaborate with families and community members, act with integrity and fairness and understand and influence the larger political, social and legal context in which they work.

For each of the standards, ISLLC identifies a series of knowledge (knowledge and understanding), disposition (beliefs, values and commitment), and performance (process and engagement) qualities for today's school leaders to embody.

Forty-four states have either adopted or adapted the ISLLC standards since they were published in 1996. Principals in those states may utilize several professional development publications, including *Standards Based Professional Development for School Leaders* containing professional development materials for school leaders, and *Collaborative Professional Development for School Leaders* providing professional development direction for schools.

Additional information may be found at www.ccsso.org/isllc.html.

Recognize the need to continually improve principals' own professional practice

Everyone who works in a learning community continually learns to improve their capacity to be effective. Professional development often centers on the teacher. But continual learning is just as important for principals. Principals can learn from other principals and should engage in as many available professional development activities as possible. It is then the responsibility of the principal to use that new information in the school, sharing best practices with classroom leaders. Online learning is now another viable source of professional development for principals.

Seeing School Culture

School culture is reflected in:

- How teachers teach

- How students experience "school"

- What is discussed in the teacher's room

- Attitudes toward work

- Stories told to visitors, newcomers

- Celebrations

Source: Robbins, P. Developed for the Region 8 Education Service Center of Northeast Indiana. For more information, visit: www.r8esc.k12.in.us.

Just as principals work with teachers to develop individual professional development plans, today's principals must develop professional development plans for themselves, involving peers, mentors and school leaders in identifying personal goals and needs. These plans serve as a guiding force for the creation and implementation of principal development activities and can directly link principal development with student achievement.

Likewise, principals benefit from the same study groups and peer engagement that teachers do. Such dialogues allow principals to identify allies and realize that they are not alone in the personal, instructional, and managerial challenges they face. Successful principals are involved in the professional development of their teachers. Attending faculty professional development activities, participating, listening and learning not only empowers the principal, but it strengthens the overall school community and builds a bridge of interest and engagement between the principal and the teacher.

Questions for Further Reflection

Learning gains have become evident to teachers as they assess students' day-to-day progress. These improvements will occur only when teacher learning is focused on clear targets for student learning and when we apply what we know about effective professional development. Principals can gauge their schools' commitment to adult learning with the following questions:

• Provide time for reflection as an important part of improving practice

How does this learning community demonstrate its commitment to the belief that reflection is an important part of the process of improvement? How often do I, as principal, take the opportunity to reflect on my own situation or on the events that are occurring in the school?

• Invest in teacher learning

Is the content knowledge of teachers being deepened by the professional development they participate in? How do we, as a school community, assess our learning? Do teachers and other instructional staff see themselves as responsible for student learning? Do they see themselves as being responsible for the learning of other adults in the school? How do teachers demonstrate their commitment to taking responsibility for their own learning?

• Connect professional development to school learning goals

Do we remain in agreement that we are committed to the belief that all of our students can learn? Does the school have a set of learning goals for students? For adults? Are these goals communicated to the entire school community? How is the creation of the school's professional development plan tied to the learning goals? How is the professional development itself evaluated in regard to student performance? What are the results of professional development activities on the practice of teachers?

• Provide opportunities for teachers to work, plan and think together

How are teachers learning from each other throughout the school day? What opportunities are provided for this learning? What opportunities do teachers have to work with and learn from each other outside of the school day? How does the principal participate in grade-level or subject-area teams? How does the rest of the staff perceive the principal's participation?

• Recognize the need to continually improve principals' own professional practice

What opportunities am I, as principal, making for my own professional development? How much time do I spend in any given week or month in thinking about how to improve my instructional and managerial capabilities as a way to continue to support the growth of others in the school community? How do I assess whether I am learning?

Standard Four Strategies

Use the Questions for Further Reflection to help you think about and rate the degree to which each Standards Four strategy is evident in your school or your practice as a school leader.

1 – Not evident in my school/practice

2 – Somewhat or occasionally evident in school/practice

3 – Consistently evident in school/practice

4 – Consistently evident, with practices that elaborate upon or exceed expectation

Self-Assessment: Beginning of the Year

	1	2	3	4
Provide time for reflection as an important part of improving practice				
Invest in teacher learning				
Connect professional development to school learning goals				
Provide opportunities for teachers to work, plan and think together				
Recognize the need to continually improve principals' own professional practice				

Self-Assessment: Middle of the Year

	1	2	3	4
Provide time for reflection as an important part of improving practice				
Invest in teacher learning				
Connect professional development to school learning goals				
Provide opportunities for teachers to work, plan and think together				
Recognize the need to continually improve principals' own professional practice				

Self-Assessment: End of the Year

	1	2	3	4
Provide time for reflection as an important part of improving practice				
Invest in teacher learning				
Connect professional development to school learning goals				
Provide opportunities for teachers to work, plan and think together				
Recognize the need to continually improve principals' own professional practice				

For More Information

Resources From NAESP:

Essentials for Principals: How To Interview, Hire and Retain High-Quality New Teachers (2000).

On the Web:

The **Standards for School Leaders** (www.ccsso.org/isllc.html) from the Interstate School Leaders Licensure Consortium (ISLLC) are available online with an introduction and comments on the standards.

The **National Staff Development Council's** Web contains:

• Standards for Staff Development (www.nsdc.org/standards.htm)

• A library of topics for educators from A to Z, including principals' role in professional development, mentoring and coaching (www.nsdc.org/library.htm)

The **ERIC Clearinghouse** (www.ericsp.org) on Teaching and Teacher Education offers rich research on teaching and practical resources for teachers.

From the Research:

Blase, J. and J. Blase. *Empowering Teachers: What Successful Principals Do.* Thousand Oaks, CA: Corwin Press, 2000.

Joyce, B. and B. Showers. *Student Achievement Through Staff Development: Fundamentals of School Renewal.* White Plains, NY: Longman Publishing Group, 1995

National Staff Development Council. "Learning To Lead, Leading To Learn: Improving School Quality Through Principal Professional Development." Special Report. Oxford, OH: NSDC, December 2000.

National Staff Development Council. *Standards for Staff Development.* Oxford, OH: NSDC, revised 2001.

Wald, P. and M. Castleberry. *Educators as Learners: Creating a Professional Learning Community in Your School.* Alexandria, VA: Association for Supervision and Curriculum Development, 2000.

Standard Five: Use Multiple Sources of Data as Diagnostic Tools

Effective principals use multiple sources of data as diagnostic tools to assess, identify and apply instructional improvement.

Effective school leaders are hunters, gatherers and consumers of information. They use every bit of information they can find to help assess where students are in relation to standards and school learning goals. Skilled principals lead their school communities in collecting, interpreting and using data to assess student achievement and factors that affect it. They know how to communicate the meaning of data and lead the school community in using data constructively to improve teaching and learning.

In the past, some schools and districts have collected data because it was an administrative requirement, not a method for making instructional improvements. Principals and teachers generally were not accustomed to looking deep into the data to evaluate their own practice and diagnose improvements. But in this era of heightened accountability and high-stakes tests, test scores are often the single evaluative measure of a school's performance. In this context, schools and principals need to pay closer attention to targeting areas for improvement in student and teacher performance.

In their focus on improving achievement, effective school leaders use multiple sources of information to assess performance, diagnose specific areas for improvement, design effective classroom lessons, make decisions about the school's goals and professional development opportunities and adapt best practices from other successful schools and teachers.

Principals' Voices:

"Staff needs to knows how to analyze student achievement data for instructional planning purposes so that each teacher is a diagnostic teacher."

What would it look like if principals were using data as a tool for decision-making? We'd see principals who:

- **Consider a variety of data sources to measure performance**

- **Analyze data using a variety of strategies**

- **Use data as tools to identify barriers to success, design strategies for improvement and plan daily instruction**

- **Benchmark successful schools with similar demographics to identify strategies for improving student achievement**

- **Create a school environment that is comfortable using data**

Consider a variety of data sources to measure performance

One of the most significant issues the principal faces is how to measure a student's progress in the classroom. Effective leaders recognize that students have differing needs for instructional time and approaches to learn at high levels. Multiple forms of data — both numerical and qualitative — are useful in creating a more fair and complete picture of student progress.

Using multiple measures of progress allows a school to do what Grant Wiggins suggests in his book, *Assessing Student Performance: Exploring the Purpose and Limits of Testing*: "Assess the student's accomplishments and progress, not merely the total score that results from points subtracted from a collection of items."

Although standardized test data is the most common measure of performance, such numerical data should be augmented by quantitative data generated in the classroom. Effective principals help their school communities see the value of using both numerical, or hard, data (including norm-referenced and standards-based test scores and performance assessments) and qualitative, or soft, data (including portfolios, student work, interviews, observations and grades) to assess performance and plan instruction.

Portfolios are an example of measuring a student's progress over time with multiple forms of information. With writing samples, norm- and standards-based test scores and a student's own reflections about his or her learning, a portfolio can provide a more complete picture of a student's accomplishments than can an isolated standardized test score.

1 Leadership | **2** Vision | **3** Student Learning | **4** Adult Learning | **5** Data & Decision-Making | **6** Community Engagement

57

Focus on Practice:

Teachers as Researchers

Thomas Metcalf School, Illinois

At Thomas Metcalf School, teachers are researchers. A K-8 lab school with 500 students and a diverse population on the Illinois State University campus, Metcalf includes in its mission a commitment to conducting research to drive and evaluate how students are learning.

Principal Glenn Schlichting believes that the buck stops with him. "I feel strongly that the principal is the key to school improvement. I am responsible for how our students perform." One of the ways he helps students and teachers perform better is to support action research, which he defines as "research that is done in context of a classroom and the school to guide our practice. It produces information that is fluid and can be used to make improvements."

He adds: "As we implement new programs and strategies, we want to find out if they're working. Research helps us answer the key question: 'How is student performance impacted by our changes in behaviors and strategies?'"

Metcalf staff members designed action research programs to answer that question about the new Everyday Math program. Test results are augmented by interviews to guage students' mathematical understanding as well as changes in teachers' teaching and belief systems.

To measure the effect of a significant infusion of new reading materials for first-graders and training for their parents, teachers designed an action research project to answer the question: "Can we improve the success of first-grade readers through the creation of an effective school-home partnership that uses books appropriately selected for the students' reading levels?"

Data were collected about student reading levels and the number of books read at home during the week. Results thus far have demonstrated that students read an average of more than 19 books each week, a nearly 600 percent increase from years before the implementation of the program. Pre- and post-testing also showed that the first-graders increased their reading levels by approximately 500 percent. The average first-grader ended the year reading beyond the third-grade level.

Principals' Voices:

"Currently, our district is beginning to learn how to use electronic data about student achievement to make decisions about children and programming. This is scary for our teachers. They fear that their students' test results will drive their evaluations. So right now I have to help them understand the power of electronic data analysis while setting aside their fears."

Focus on Practice:
Instructional Facilitators Support Teachers' Use of Data
Buchanan Elementary School, Pennsylvania

Buchanan Elementary School Principal Debra Leese and Instructional Facilitator Diane Butzer have a unique partnership, in which Leese sets the vision and expectations for improvements in student achievement and directs teachers to use Butzer's assistance to help them get there.

Every school in Lancaster has an instructional facilitator, who leads the school's professional development and spends one day a week in intense district-level training, most of it focused on assessment and using data.

At Buchanan Elementary, a K-5 school with 400 students, Butzer is also the person in the school who examines data, looks for trends and helps teachers find ways to address problem areas. She has prepared class profiles for all of the teachers so they can see exactly where students are in each content area and then help to target schoolwide issues as well as classroom-specific issues.

In her examination of the data, Butzer might see that fourth-grade students haven't performed well on reading comprehension two years in a row. Butzer would then help the fourth-grade teachers — in their weekly grade-level meeting with her — see that trend and figure out how to change their instruction so that students better comprehend and interpret what they read. She might do that by demonstrating teaching methods or lessons that build comprehension skills.

"As an instructional facilitator, I'm in classrooms every day modeling the instruction that produces the results we want on the assessments. I don't evaluate teachers; I'm 'in the trenches' with them," says Butzer. "My job is to help teachers analyze the regular district assessments to determine students' strengths and weaknesses and then help them figure out what needs to be taught to get kids to a higher level."

She helps parents understand standardized test results at a general session during parent/teacher conferences to help them look critically at the scores and understand what that means for what their children will be working on in school. She is also available for individual meetings with parents to discuss their child's test results.

Analyze data using a variety of strategies

Effective principals help their school communities more fully understand the meaning of surface data. Three data analysis strategies are particularly important for making meaning of data: disaggregation, drilling down and examining trends.

Disaggregating data — breaking apart big data chunks by student and school characteristics or by grade levels or classrooms — is important in targeting the instructional needs of all students. Principals must insist that their school communities use data in disaggregated ways; looking at averages will only give schools limited information, which in turn yields only average strategies. Instead, schools need rich information and excellent strategies. For instance, breaking apart test data according to ethnicity or eligibility for free or reduced-price lunch is one way to pinpoint particular groups of students who aren't receiving the instruction they need to succeed.

The process of "drilling down" into data means looking more deeply into data and making useful comparisons between data points. University of Connecticut education professor Phillip Streifer writes in *School Administrator*, "The drill-down process starts with a global question or issue, which then is broken down into its component parts for analysis. Once the analysis is completed, all the data are considered from one's 'helicopter view' to make reasoned decision on next steps." Drilling down entails looking at the many factors that affect performance to analyze the underlying reasons for what the surface data tell us.

Looking for trends, or patterns, in the data over time is also helpful in targeting specific areas that show success or need for improvement. For example, a school could monitor the effectiveness of a math or science program by watching for trends in student performance from one year to the next and comparing that information to the baseline data from before the program started. Looking at such trends is much more informative than simply reporting one year's numbers.

Use data as tools to identify barriers to success, design strategies for improvement and plan daily instruction

Data becomes useful when people understand what the information means and how to apply it to determine successes, diagnose problems and plan action. By using data as an information source for regular assessment of students and school programs, effective school leaders encourage a view of data as a diagnostic tool rather than a punitive means of pointing out failures.

Effective principals use data as an information source to regularly assess student progress and make decisions about classroom instruction. They work with teachers to examine test scores, student work and other forms of data to determine what students need to perform at high levels.

Principals' Voices:

"We are working to understand the importance of the examination of student performance data, whether through norm-referenced tests, criterion-referenced tests, authentic assessments, and the list goes on. Further, this reflection piece provides the opportunity for staff to triangulate data which may also include surveys completed by parents and students of the school."

Effective school leaders support the use of data as a diagnostic tool by doing the following:

- Making time for teachers to work together or with a school data coach to examine data and discuss what the information means

- Encouraging teachers to use data to evaluate their own instruction

- Giving teachers strategies to use data to plan lessons and make decisions about classroom instruction

- Sharing ideas about successful practices that may contribute to higher levels of performance in certain areas

- Designing professional development opportunities for teachers based on needs for greater content area knowledge or pedagogical strategies as identified by the data

Focus on Practice:

Data Drives Design and Evaluation of Successful Literacy Program
Washington Intermediate School, Illinois

Using research and multiple forms of data to design instructional activities and continually evaluate progress is an integral part of Washington Intermediate School's vision statement. Staying true to that vision, Principal Brad Hutchison and his team created a school action plan using several forms of data to address a trend of low reading comprehension and writing scores over time across several grade levels.

"We can't depend on year-old data. We need to be targeting students based on current data that assesses where a student is at this point in time. A lot can happen in a year, or even three months, with a child's learning," says Hutchison. To address students' writing skills, Hutchison had a classroom teacher lead the school in developing rubrics for good writing and in making available strong writing samples at each grade level to help teachers and students know what is attainable.

Teachers measure progress every trimester and students evaluate their own progress at the end of the school year with standards-based "I can do it" self-evaluation forms and with the evidence in their portfolios.

"Most schools collect [test, attendance, and transcript] data to satisfy administrative requirements rather than to assess and evaluate school or student improvement. Educators rarely examine these data in a systemic way to assess the quality of teaching and learning at their school."

Theodore Creighton (2001)

Types and Sources of Data

Numerical (Hard) Data:

All sources of hard data are measured in numbers. Tests that produce hard data are often administered from sources external to the school.

- Norm-referenced tests compare students to one another, based on a "norm"

- Standards-based (or criterion-referenced) tests measure student progress toward attaining standards or another set of criteria

- Performance-based assessments give students questions requiring some kind of performance and multiple choice tests

- Characteristics of the school population, including breakdowns of ethnicity and race, mobility of students and staff, and participation in free and reduced-priced meals program

Qualitative (Soft) Data:

Sources of soft data produce qualitative information about perceptions, attitudes and behaviors. Often this information is school- or classroom-based.

- Student portfolios and other collections of student work

- Classroom grades

- Interviews with students, teachers, administrators or families

- Observation of students and teachers and descriptive evaluations of what was observed

- Surveys that provide information on parent satisfaction, climate or students' health and social service needs

- Behavioral rubrics of attendance, referrals, detention, retention and positive behaviors

Benchmark successful schools with similar demographics to identify strategies for improving student achievement

Effective school leaders "benchmark" schools with similar resources and student composition in their quest for instructional practices that can improve student performance. They look for schools that are excelling in areas where they may be ineffective and seek out ways to replicate these schools' best practices.

Several benchmarking efforts across the country show that it is possible for schools to succeed with a large percentage of poor and minority students. These efforts essentially say that the socio-economic status of students need not determine how successful the school can be. A high level of performance in high-need schools is possible.

For instance, an Illinois principal whose school consistently produces low reading and writing scores can find successful schools of similar demographics by using the Illinois School Improvement Web site (http://ilsi.isbe.net). They can then seek out information about the strategies those schools use to help their students excel in reading and writing.

Create a school environment that is comfortable using data

As the school leader, it is the principal's role to create a common understanding of what data is in the first place, and to create a school environment that is comfortable with studying and using data. Effective school leaders show they are willing to immerse themselves in data before asking their staff to do the same. They show they are committed to using data for constructive purposes. And they lead efforts to present data simply and clearly, in formats that are meaningful to faculty, parents and community members.

Many teachers have not had the experience, either in their training programs or in practice, of looking at their own performance in relation to how students are doing. As well, few parents are comfortable with data and the statistical calculations that are associated with the term. Effective principals alleviate fears around data, explain what the data mean and facilitate of teachers' and parents' efforts to gather, understand and use data to improve student learning.

In this way, principals create a willingness among the school community to take a close look at the school's successes and challenges, reflect on what they see and take greater responsibility for building on what's working and improve what isn't.

Examples of Data-Driven School Improvement Planning Models

- Onward to Excellence II (based on Effective Schools research) teaches school leaders the process of using data to develop a profile of school performance that will then set the school mission and goals. Onward to Excellence training is delivered by the Northwest Regional Education Laboratory. For more information, see www.nwrel.org/scpd/ote.

- Illinois Technology and Leadership for Change (ITLC) provides data-driven school improvement training for Illinois principals that uses frameworks and tools from the ISLLC standards, Baldrige Criteria for Education Excellence, and technology for making data-driven decisions. ITLC is one of the 50 Bill and Melinda Gates Foundation challenge grants for school leadership and technology development. For more information, see www.sadi.ilstu.edu or contact ITLC Project Coordinators Lynda Irvin (leirvin@ilstu.edu) or Julie Schlichting (jas127@juno.com).

- Koalaty Kid is an approach to school improvement that applies the principles of total quality as used by the business community. Koalaty Kid training and publications offer a comprehensive theory, a system for partnering with local business, a process for developing improvement strategies, and an extensive set of tools for organizing and analyzing data. For more information, see www.koalatykid.org or call the American Association for Quality (800-248-1946).

- DataWorks Educational Research offers online tutorials for its Targeted Improvement Model that eliminates the socio-economic components schools can't control and concentrates on factors which schools can control. On its Web site, DataWorks outlines its five-step process of collecting, analyzing and using data to create a targeted improvement plan. Sample action plans and evaluation plans are available. For more information, see www.dataworks2.com.

Principals' Voices:

"Principals not only need to lead their schools' efforts in analyzing data, they also need to visit classrooms and help teachers use data to determine what needs to be taught."

Questions for Further Reflection

With the following questions, school leaders can determine their own and their school's use of data to assess student and teacher performance and use that information to make improvements.

• Consider a variety of data sources to measure performance

How do I lead the school community in using data from multiple sources to measure student performance and evaluate the effective of our programs? Do we augment the use of hard, numerical test data with soft data such as student work to pinpoint specific areas where students need additional help?

• Analyze data using a variety strategies

In what ways do we disaggregate our data? What strategies do we use to look deeper into the surface data of standardized test scores? What additional data or data analyses methods would help us look at underlying factors for low and high achievement? Do we examine our test and other data for trends in student or teacher performance?

• Use data as tools to identify barriers to success, design strategies for improvement and plan daily instruction

Do I make time for teachers to look at and reflect on data together? How do we use data to plan lessons and make decisions about instructional programs? Do I observe classrooms to assure teachers are using data to determine if students are mastering what is taught? Do I use subject-area and grade-level achievement data to design professional development?

• Benchmark successful schools with similar demographics to identify strategies for improving student achievement

Do I seek out information about strategies used in high-performing schools with similar characteristics to my school? How do I help my teachers replicate best practices in their classrooms?

• Create a school environment that is comfortable using data

How do I convey to my school community the importance of studying and using data? How do I include teachers, parents and the community in the discussion and interpretation of data? Are my staff members wary of data, or are they willing to immerse themselves in the information? In what ways do I ensure that data about my school are presented clearly in formats staff and families can easily understand?

Standard Five Strategies

Use the Questions for Further Reflection to help you think about and rate the degree to which each Standard Five strategy is evident in your school or your practice as a school leader.

1 – Not evident in my school/practice

2 – Somewhat or occasionally evident in school/practice

3 – Consistently evident in school/practice

4 – Consistently evident, with practices that elaborate upon or exceed expectation

Self-Assessment: Beginning of the Year

	1	2	3	4
Consider a variety of data sources to measure performance				
Analyze data using a variety of strategies				
Use data as tools to identify barriers to success, design strategies for improvement and plan daily instruction				
Benchmark successful schools with similar demographics to identify strategies for improving student achievement				
Create a school environment that is comfortable using data				

Self-Assessment: Middle of the Year

	1	2	3	4
Consider a variety of data sources to measure performance				
Analyze data using a variety of strategies				
Use data as tools to identify barriers to success, design strategies for improvement and plan daily instruction				
Benchmark successful schools with similar demographics to identify strategies for improving student achievement				
Create a school environment that is comfortable using data				

Self-Assessment: End of the Year

	1	2	3	4
Consider a variety of data sources to measure performance				
Analyze data using a variety of strategies				
Use data as tools to identify barriers to success, design strategies for improvement and plan daily instruction				
Benchmark successful schools with similar demographics to identify strategies for improving student achievement				
Create a school environment that is comfortable using data				

For More Information

Resources From NAESP:

Essentials for Principals: Meeting the Challenges of High-Stakes Testing (2001).

Essentials for Principals: Data-Based Decision-Making (2001).

On the Web:

The North Central Regional Educational Laboratory's Toolbelt
(www.ncrel.org/toolbelt) is full of information gathering tools — ranging from checklists to surveys, paper-and-pencil to software — to help educators collect data about their classroom, school or district, professional practice or community need. The site also features stories about successful data-driven decision making and an eight-step model for incorporating data into school improvement plans.

Several Web sites contain state- and school-level data for the purposes of benchmarking and school improvement planning, including:

• **The Maryland School Improvement Web site** (www.mdk12.org)

• **The Illinois School Improvement Web site** (http://ilsi.isbe.net)

• **Just for the Kids** (www.just4kids.org) in Texas

Look for the same kinds of data and comparison tools on Web sites from state departments of education, local newspapers and business groups.

From the Research:

American Association of School Administrators. *Data-Driven Decisions: New Ways To Get Answers.* No. 4. Vol. 58. *The School Administrator.* Arlington, VA: AASA, April 2001.

The Education Trust. *Community Data Guide.* Washington, DC: The Education Trust.

Holcomb, E. L. *Getting Excited About Data: How to Combine People, Passion and Proof.* Thousand Oaks, CA: Corwin Press, 1999.

Wiggins, G. P. *Assessing Student Performance: Exploring the Purpose and Limits of Testing.* San Francisco: Jossey Bass, 1993.

Standard Six: Actively Engage the Community

Effective principals actively engage the community to create shared responsibility for student and school success.

Schools and communities are inextricably intertwined, and the principal is the linchpin in creating a learning community that seamlessly integrates the work and expectations of students, teachers, parents, citizens, community and business leaders and policymakers.

Public schools are public institutions, embodying the values and hopes of the community. Public schools play a key role as a model of democracy at work in our society. They do so by demonstrating that all students should have the opportunity to learn at high levels, regardless of where they are born, and by preparing them for equal chances at success as citizens and in life.

Public schools are, by definition, owned by the public. Parents, business leaders and other citizens have a stake in the product of public schools; they also have a say in decisions that affect the schools in their community. Effective principals understand that they must engage the entire community in conversations and decisions about the school. They promote two-way conversations where both sides are listening and acting. And they help the community define their role and responsibility for public education.

Communities have an expectation that schools will be safe places that are efficiently managed. They want to know that their tax dollars are being well-spent on a quality education for their children. They want the buses to run on time and healthy food to be served in the cafeteria. And they often expect schools to address problems of childcare, healthcare and other issues beyond their historic charge.

Principals' Voices:

"Principals need processes that work in bringing in the community, including parents, to be involved in meaningful and supportive activities."

What would it look like if a school were effectively engaging families and the community? We'd see principals who:

> • **Engage the community to build greater ownership for the work of the school**
>
> • **Share leadership and decision-making**
>
> • **Encourage parents to become meaningfully involved in the school and in their own children's learning**
>
> • **Ensure that students and families are connected to the health, human and social services they need to stay focused on learning**

Engage the community to build greater ownership for the work of the school

Greater understanding of and involvement in the serious business of schools leads to greater ownership of schools. With greater ownership, the public is more willing to commit time, resources and votes needed for long-term investments in education.

As a leader in the effort to build greater ownership of schools, the effective principal engages the broad community in setting and carrying out the vision and goals of the school. As Ernesto Cortes, Jr. of the Industrial Areas Foundation says, the principal's challenge is to become the leader of a team where the "public are the leaders in education reform."

Sometimes engaging the public simply means keeping them informed of school and student performance. Principals must be willing to tell the bad news along with the good. They must be willing to explain to the community reasons behind what the data say and what is in place to address problems and build on successes.

Focus on Practice:
Preparing Young People for Life
Carver Middle School, Mississippi

For today's students, school is more than just books and computers. It is about the people — teachers, administrators and others — who serve as a constant in their lives, preparing them for both academic and social success.

At Carver Middle School, providing lessons in social and emotional behaviors is just as important as teaching multiplication tables. Principal Edward Wiggins is committed to providing students the confidence, sense of responsibility and academic preparation they will need to lead the community in years to come.

In Raymond, Mississippi, Carver students are encouraged to participate in extracurricular activities that teach the importance of teamwork, leadership and practice. Students are involved in a variety of clubs and teams including a Junior Beta Club honor society, student council, band and basketball.

"Education involves working with the whole child," Wiggins said. "Students can get excited by what the world offers, by what types of activities they are provided in school."

Field trips are organized to educate students on everything from their local community to proper etiquette in social situations to career options. Community leaders volunteer their time as role models and mentors to the 425 students at the predominantly African-American school.

Carver students have taken responsibility for their own actions. Students at the rural Mississippi school have created the appropriate consequences — from informing a parent to standing before the entire school to explain one's actions — that are applied when school rules are broken by a fellow student.

To aid the school in the development of these programs, Wiggins has turned to Title I funding to provide motivational materials that help students and faculty engage in lessons on character development, self-esteem, perseverance, work ethic and honesty.

"We are preparing them for the actual world of work. These are all common sense kinds of things for children," Wiggins said. "We practice the things we want them to do."

Principals' Voices:

"We're in the schools doing a fantastic job, but that's not what the public hears. So it's up to us to let the community know exactly what is going on in the schools."

A principal committed to public engagement understands that the community needs avenues to learn about and reflect on academic standards, the school's goals, how the school is using its resources and what the data shows about the school's progress. Although true public engagement in schools is powerful, it is time-consuming and complicated. It requires ongoing collaboration and communication. When done well, though, all members of the community share the responsibility and authority for creating a successful school.

Teachers are a particularly important part of a school's engagement effort. As the most visible and often most respected people in education, teachers frequently have a role in communicating with the public and key community stakeholders.

Focus on Practice
A Full-Service Community School
Rodney B. Cox Elementary School, Florida

Dental care. Counseling. Healthcare. Adult education. In large cities, many of these services can be found in local community centers. But in Dade City, Florida, a semi-rural, small town, all can be found at Rodney B. Cox Elementary School, a preK-5 school with 512 students.

The school provides quality instruction for its diverse student population (34 percent African-American, 55 percent Hispanic,10 percent White; 93 percent of students are eligible for free or reduced-price lunch.

In the pursuit of improved student performance, school Principal Leila Mizer faced a real challenge. With many parents lacking transportation and telephones and generally negative in their perception of schools, how could Cox involve parents in classroom activity?

The answer was simpler than one might think. Mizer used one of the school's most valuable assets — the school staff — to aid in the construction of a relationship between the school and community. Bilingual teachers provided translation for Spanish-speaking families at school events and activities. Teachers made quarterly home visits to parents, updating them on student and school performance. And Mizer encouraged parents to visit the school regularly — for meetings with teachers, to observe or even just for lunch.

Today, Rodney B. Cox Elementary School serves as a strong example of commitment to the community. By educating and serving parents and students alike, Cox has redefined the full-service school.

Share leadership and decision-making

Some schools have formal structures for shared decision-making, often called site-based management. Under this structure, principals assume a new role as facilitator and leader of a group of people that sets the course for the school. The successful principal instills leadership capacity into these site councils, giving them authority to be full participants in decisions about policy, budget, programs and instructional improvements. This requires shifting traditional lines of authority to take advantage of the unique skills and perspectives this leadership team brings to the learning community.

Focus on Practice:
Building Bridges to Spanish-Speaking Families
Talent Elementary School, Oregon

"Estamos constantemente aprendiendo y explorando. We are constantly learning and exploring," exclaims the staff, students and families of Talent Elementary School in both Spanish and English. Nestled in the hills of Southern Oregon, Talent Elementary with 490 students boasts a "state of the art" two-way immersion program now in its eighth year.

When the Spanish-speaking student population jumped from 9 percent to 18 percent in three years, Principal Jeff Fagan encouraged the school to re-examine all of its approaches to teaching and learning. Knowing that family involvement is a critical factor for school success, the school and the PTA developed an intensive effort called "Los Puentes – Bridges" to involve Spanish-speaking families in their children's education.

First the school listened carefully to the needs of the community and discovered that Latino families lacked the basic information they needed to help their children – both in academics and in the logistics of getting to and succeeding in school. Los Puentes worked with the school board to ensure that all communications were translated appropriate for every family in the community. Attendance at PTA meetings soared. Families were more connected to community resources geared toward Latinos. And students had the support they needed from their families.

"We're beginning to build some trust here," explains Fagan. "We can't expect people to be involved in schools unless we value and respect them."

> "To involve parents and citizens in the work of schools is to make them partners in decision-making. To make diverse constituencies partners in school improvements is to say that the outcome of that process will be something that the partners can support and agree on."
>
> Annenberg Institute on Public Engagement (1998)

Encourage parents to become meaningfully involved in the school and in their own children's learning

Principals' everyday experiences, along with more than 30 years of research, illustrate the critical nature of family involvement in children's success.

Principals can help families understand the importance of their role in student learning. They set a vision for what it means for families to be a part of the learning community.

In this vision, they provide the information parents need to boost their children's academic success. They encourage parent leaders to share these tools with other parents. Principals and teachers create a school where families feel welcome by regularly inviting parents into the building.

True learning communities draw parents into the learning culture, assessing their needs and providing information and training where needed. Unused classrooms or obscure hallways become parent resource centers with books, videos and places to connect with other parents and teachers. Materials are provided in multiple languages and reflect the diversity of the school population.

Beyond welcoming families, schools encourage family involvement by reaching out to families through home visits, connections with faith communities and personal invitations.

To fully support a child's academic success, parents need an understanding of the high standards expected of their children. Schools build this understanding through workshops, back-to-school nights, newsletters, Web sites and other communications that emphasize the academic work of the school.

Organizing a Standards-Based Back-to-School Night

Standards-based education can help all students succeed but only if parents and educators understand how it works. Back-to-school night is a critical opportunity to educate parents and the community on standards and school culture. A principal's guidelines for planning a standards-based back-to-school night include:

1. Start recruiting parents to come
2. Prepare teachers and their classrooms ahead of time
3. Prepare an overview on standards
4. Focus on student work
5. Avoid jargon
6. Provide refreshments and opportunities for parents to ask questions
7. Get feedback from parents

For hands-on tools to help create a standards-based back-to-school night, visit www.publicengagement.com/tools/standards/engaging/en_backtoschool.htm

Six Types of Parent Involvement

Explaining the power of effective parent involvement on academic achievement, Joyce Epstein directs the Center for Schools, Communities and Families at Johns Hopkins University in Baltimore, Maryland.

Her framework of six types of involvement helps educators develop more comprehensive programs of school-family-community partnerships:

1. Parenting: Assist families with parenting and child-rearing skills, understanding child and adolescent development and setting home conditions that support children as students at each age and grade level. Assist schools in understanding families

2. Communicating: Communicate with families about school programs and student progress through effective school-to-home and home-to-school communications

3. Volunteering: Improve recruitment, training, work and schedules to involve families as volunteers and audiences at the school or in other locations to support students and school programs

4. Learning at Home: Involve families with their children in learning activities at home, including homework and other curriculum-linked activities and decisions

5. Decision-Making: Include families as participants in school decisions, governance and advocacy through PTA/PTO, school councils, committees and other parent organizations

6. Collabrating With the Community: Coordinate resources and services for families, students and the school with businesses, agencies, and other groups, and provide services to the community

For more information: www.csos.jhu.edu/p2000/sixtypes.htm

Source: Epstein, J.L., Coates, L., Salinas, K.C., Sanders, M.G. and Simon, B.S. *School, Family and Community Partnerships: Your Handbook for Action.* Thousand Oaks, CA: Corwin Press, 1997.

Principals' Voices

"Parents listen to me and accept me because of my relationships with their children. That's the way to involve parents."

Principals'
Voices

"As a leader in
my community, I
am helping shape
opinions and
craft policies.
That experience
and knowledge
stretches me and
my teachers and
helps move us
forward in our
work."

Tips for Working With Policy Makers

These tips were developed from a meeting of principals and policy makers at the Principals Leadership Summit in July 2001, sponsored by the U.S. Department of Education and co-sponsored by the National Association of Elementary School Principals and the National Association of Secondary School Principals.

- Get to know your local school board and city/county council members and state legislators. Working with policy makers is more about relationships than a formal process of "good" lobbying; establish relationships with the goal of helping policy makers understand and respect your perspective.

- Support political candidates with your time and money. It's important to support both local and state candidates by volunteering for their campaigns (e.g., walking door-to-door, distributing flyers) and contributing money (if only in small amounts).

- Work with legislators in both political parties. Good education legislation requires bipartisan support to be passed.

- Make your case regarding changes in policy or proposed legislation by a) offering solutions rather than complaining and b) presenting research that supports your perspective. For instance, when making an argument against high-stakes tests (or another policy that is not educationally sound), explain what doesn't work about it, why, and what groups of students and/or teachers that aren't benefiting as a result.

- Invite local opinion leaders, school board members, city/county officials and state legislators into your school. Help them see education policy in practice and other factors that show what works or why a policy needs to be changed. If policy makers have direct experience with policy, both good and bad, they are more likely to see and advocate for your perspective.

- Find allied community and state groups to educate policy makers on educators' concerns and advocate for reasonable, effective education legislation. Coalitions of interests are more able to get things done than single voices.

- Mobilize constituents to share their views on reasonable education legislation with policy makers. Numbers equal power. When people show up at public meetings, sign letters and make phone calls, policy makers are more likely to listen to the message.

Ensure that students and families are connected to the health, human and social services they need to stay focused on learning

Participants in a learning community know that until the basic needs of food, shelter and health are met, little learning can take place. A caring principal is an advocate for the students who arrive at school with so many barriers in their personal lives that learning is virtually impossible.

With extensive academic requirements, schools are hard-pressed to stretch their staff and resources to provide children with needed services. Effective school leaders will seek help from the community to coordinate health and social services with local providers. At one end of the spectrum, a principal will encourage the development of a full-service school with extensive services on-site with a full-time coordinator. At the other, a principal would help create methods for faculty and staff to help families access the community resources they need.

"Young people do not live in a cocoon."

Joy Dryfoos (1998)

Focus on Practice:
A Safe Place for Learning
George Mason Elementary School, Virginia

Creating a safe and comfortable environment for learning is a high priority at George Mason Elementary in Alexandria, Virginia. "Being safe is a new reality," notes Principal Lois Berlin. "We have to implement prevention and intervention programs that support and nurture children."

At this urban-suburban school with 300 students, character education pulls together all of the other school safety efforts. The diverse student population is now 45 percent white, 35 percent Latino and 12 percent African-American and has changed significantly over the past few years. With new immigrant, mostly Spanish-speaking families always joining the community, the school staff understands that this is not something else on their plates, but it is the foundation of the school's culture.

Respect is a key element of the school environment. "Issues of bullying and prejudice have no place here," emphasizes Berlin. She continually reinforces this message in a positive way. Students can write in a "Random Acts of Kindness Book" in the front office when they witness good or responsible behaviors. Staff and student talk about what it means to learn in a safe environment.

The school is assessing its efforts in character education through numerous methods, including questionnaires, number of office reports, attendance and participation in after-school programs. For now, the school staff is working hard toward their goal that children grow up safe, embrace diversity, solve conflict peacefully, choose safe habits for living and exhibit positive character in each decision they make.

Questions for Further Reflection

To gauge the extent and effectiveness of engagement efforts in the work of the school, principals can use the following guiding questions.

• Engage the community to build greater ownership for the work of the school

Do I talk about standards and high expectations for students with parents? Am I in ongoing conversations with various sectors of the community? Do I have a regular vehicle for communication, like e-mail or a newsletter? Am I honest and forthcoming in sharing information about school challenges? Have I recognized a community member for their contributions lately?

• Share leadership and decision-making

Am I practicing shared leadership? Do community members truly have a voice at the decision-making table? Am I listening carefully to parents and the community? Do I include representative members of the community in major decisions? Do I reach out to those not often involved in the school?

• Encourage parents to become more meaningfully involved in their school and in their own children's learning

Am I creating a welcoming school climate for parents? Do I reach out to parents not actively involved in the school? Do I understand the language and cultural barriers parents face? Am I providing resources and tools to help parents be closely involved in their children's education?

• Ensure that students and families are connected to the health, human and social services they need to stay focused on learning.

Do I know the right people to call for healthcare solutions, abusive situations, psychiatric services? Do I help create structures that connect students to social services they need? Have I considered more formal connections with health and social services?

Standard Six Strategies

Use the Questions for Further Reflection to help you think about and rate the degree to which each Standard Six strategy is evident in your school or your practice as a school leader.

1 – Not evident in my school/practice

2 – Somewhat or occasionally evident in school/practice

3 – Consistently evident in school/practice

4 – Consistently evident, with practices that elaborate upon or exceed expectation

Self-Assessment: Beginning of the Year

	1	2	3	4
Engage the community to build greater ownership for the work of the school				
Share leadership and decision-making				
Encourage parents to become meaningfully involved in the school and in their own children's learning				
Ensure that students and families are connected to the health, human and social services they need to stay focused on learning				

Self-Assessment: Middle of the Year

	1	2	3	4
Engage the community to build greater ownership for the work of the school				
Share leadership and decision-making				
Encourage parents to become meaningfully involved in the school and in their own children's learning				
Ensure that students and families are connected to the health, human and social services they need to stay focused on learning				

Self-Assessment: End of the Year

	1	2	3	4
Engage the community to build greater ownership for the work of the school				
Share leadership and decision-making				
Encourage parents to become meaningfully involved in the school and in their own children's learning				
Ensure that students and families are connected to the health, human and social services they need to stay focused on learning				

For More Information

Resources From NAESP:

Our Children, Our Schools, Our Future Campaign Action Kit (2000)

After-School Programs & the K-8 Principal (1999)

Early Childhood Education & the Elementary School Principal (1998)

Essentials for Principals: Strengthening the Connection Between School and Home (2001)

On the Web:

The Partnership for Family Involvement in Education (http://pfie.ed.gov) offers a database of more than 6,000 members and several publications on strong partnerships among schools, families, businesses and community and religious groups.

Afterschool.gov (www.afterschool.gov) features tools for starting running and funding afterschool programs, planning activities and linking with community partners.

The Coalition for Community Schools (www.communityschools.org) offers more than 20 approaches to building strong partnerships with families and community residents to develop quality education, youth development, family support and community development.

The Public Education Network (www.publiceducation.org) features easy-to-use tools and resources from community-based initiatives that involve communities in the work of improving public schools through teacher quality, standards and accountability and school/community partnerships.

The National PTA features a parent involvement section (www.pta.org/parentinvolvement) with several tools, including tips and Q&As that explain in simple language ways and reasons for parents to get involved in their children's education.

From the Research:

Annenberg Institute for School Reform. *Reasons for Hope, Voices for Change*. Providence, RI: Brown University, 1998.

Dryfoos, J. *Safe Passage Making It Through Adolescence in a Risky Society: What Parents, Schools and Communities Can Do*. Oxford, UK: Oxford University Press, 1998.

Mathews, D. *Is There a Public for Public Schools?* Dayton, OH: Kettering Foundation Press, 1996.

U.S. Department of Education. *Family Involvement in Children's Education: Successful Local Approaches*. Available at: www.ed.gov/pubs/FamInvolve.

A Call to Action

What Principals Need To Improve Student Achievement

I f school leaders are to be held accountable for ensuring higher levels of achievement for all students, they will require more autonomy, professional development and resources to do so. Without such support, the principal's job is virtually impossible.

Here are 10 ways districts, states and the federal government can support school leaders:

1. Build principals' capacity to provide instructional leadership. Federal, state and local education agencies should promote efforts to build the capacity of principals to assure quality instruction. Principals need resources and flexibility to consider a variety of ways to emphasize instruction, including innovative ways to increase instructional time. With resources for additional staff development days and before- and after-school programs focused on academics, reading and other specialties, principals can expand and enrich instructional time. States and districts should also reconsider policies that create barriers to quality instruction, including extraneous curriculum requirements.

Guides for such policies include standards for staff development, such as those created by the National Staff Development Council, which inform decision-making about the selection of the content and learning processes for all school employees. Standards for instructional leadership, developed by the Interstate School Leaders Licensure Consortium (ISLLC) provide a framework for effective practice of principals and other instructional leaders.

2. Provide support, funds and flexibility for alternative leadership arrangements. Balancing leadership and management responsibilities requires new thinking about leadership structures in the school. First, all schools need a full-time, qualified principal. In addition, principals need co-leaders in roles of assistant principals, lead teachers, guidance counselors and administrative officers. Principals should have the flexibility to adopt leadership arrangements that best suit the needs of the staff and school community.

3. Improve working conditions. Principals need autonomy to build a staff dedicated to quality learning and the ability to significantly reward staff for strong performance. This includes examining the relationships with school boards, improving contracts and tenure arrangements and creating pension portability from one district or state to another. Principals need autonomy to develop budgets and to manage their schools according to key learning goals.

4. Improve salaries and pay structures. Principals need salaries commensurate with those of other professionals with similar responsibilities. Principals should be paid for the time, responsibility, care and knowledge they bring to the job. Principals should have financial incentives for meeting the standards outlined in this document and should have the opportunity for other rewards such as sabbaticals, advanced training or international exchanges.

5. Assess principals fairly. Principals need meaningful, fair and regular evaluation of their performance. They should not be judged solely on standardized test scores, but on a variety of measures including self-assessment, progress toward school learning goals and other indicators based on the standards for principals presented in Leading Learning Communities.

6. Demand greater accountability within established frameworks. Principals see themselves as responsible for student and adult learning. This accountability should be accompanied by adequate strategies to build capacity and provide support. Principals need to have clear understanding of the expectations for their work and how they are going to be held accountable for it.

7. Recognize and reward principals through a national certification process. Principals need recognition for their efforts, both locally and nationally. At the national level, principals need a process for national certification, similar to that provided to teachers by the National Board for Professional Teaching Standards. A national certification — based on the standards described in this guide — would provide a benchmark against which principals can compare their current practices, provide a common vocabulary for instructional improvement and give purpose and meaning to professional development.

8. Build learning opportunities and networks of principals. Just as teachers are isolated in their classrooms, so are principals often isolated in their buildings. School leaders need support and resources from other principals. Districts, states and regions should provide a means of linking effective practices in the principalship, through principal mentoring, coaching, listserves, study groups and conferences.

9. Rethink principal preparation programs. Principals need strong preparation programs that clearly define and describe the nature of instructional leadership. Principals must be extremely knowledgeable about how children learn and develop, how teachers teach, what kind of training helps teachers the most and what kind of interventions and support school leaders can provide. Most of the education that prospective principals receive occurs outside of a school context and is designed to be generic in its application, rather than being situated in specific problems of practice. Principals need preparation programs that include reflection, an expanded knowledge base regarding leadership and management and instructional strategies based on real practice. Preparation programs should be accredited by national standards, such as those of the National Council for the Accreditation of Teacher Education.

10. Develop federal policies that strengthen principals' ability to serve all students. Federal legislation that enhances student achievement and promotes excellence needs to consider the unique role of the principal in implementing these programs. For instance, Title II of the Elementary and Secondary Elementary Act needs strong language to ensure the recruitment and retention of qualified principals, as well as their ongoing professional development.

In addition, Congress should authorize an adequate level of funding for essential programs, including substantial increases for Title I and the Individuals with Disabilities Education Act (IDEA). Title I is the major federal source of extra assistance in the core subject areas to students in areas of need. The program serves only a fraction of eligible students and should be improved.

Similarly, schools are struggling to meet spiraling special education costs. As they do, they would be served by additional federal support for special education (IDEA), which has never come close to the 40 percent share authorized under the original Education of All Handicapped Children Act (PL 94-142).

Methodology

A Conversation by, of and for Principals

The National Association of Elementary School Principals asked Collaborative Communications Group, an organization concerned with public engagement in public education, to convene a process across the association to redefine the role of principals and to create standards for principal performance. The process was designed to:

- Engage NAESP members in defining quality in schools and standards for school leaders

- Identify and illuminate effective practices aligned with the principal standards

- Review drafts of the guide in relationship to NAESP objectives and for authenticity in relation to the practice of principals

- Use the creation of the standards document as a vehicle to encourage NAESP members to reflect on their practice

The nine-month process resulted in this guide, which Collaborative Communications Group wrote and revised. The process included:

- **Creation and convening of a Standards Committee.** A representative group of principals, nominated by NAESP state leaders, met in April, July and September to outline, discuss and review this guide. Throughout the nine-month process, the committee also participated in an online learning community via listserve to share reflections. Darrell Rud, the president of NAESP, chaired the committee.

- **Interviews with NAESP staff.** NAESP's executive leadership team provided critical insights on the need for, and structure and content of, this guide.

- **Research.** A review of research spanned education and organizational leadership and management, instructional practice, academic standards and public engagement.

- **Conversations/Interviews with principals.** More than 40 principals were interviewed, including those who participated in focus groups at the 2001 NAESP convention in San Diego, CA. These conversations focused on the definition of quality in schools and the role of principals in leading learning communities.

- **Participation in the National Principals Summit.** The 2001 National Principals Summit, hosted by the U.S. Department of Education, provided context on the state of the principal profession.

- **Discussion at NAESP State Leaders Conference.** The initial concept of the guide provided a framework for input and conversation at the State Leadership Conference in Washington, DC, in July 2001.

- **Review of drafts.** In addition to reviews by NAESP staff and the Standards Committee, state leaders were asked for direct input on the NAESP policy statement on instructional leadership, which appears as the introduction to this guide. Other reviewers outside NAESP, including the American Association of School Administrators, the Education Research Service, the Education Trust and others who work closely with principals, also made comments on drafts.

Committee on Standards for Principals

NAESP gratefully acknowledges the contributions of the representatives from each of the regional zones and others on the committee for their tireless energy and thoughtful reflection on the complex roles of the principal.

Mr. Darrell C. Rud
Committee Chair
NAESP President
Principal
Newman Elementary School
Billings, MT

Dr. Terry Brenner
Principal
Wilder Elementary School
Grand Forks, ND

Ms. Barbara A. Chester
Principal
Mill Park Elementary School
Portland, OR

Dr. Beth Christoff
Principal
Toth Elementary School
Perrysburg, OH

Dr. James L. Doud
Professor and Chair
Education Leadership,
Policy and Foundations
Department of Education
University of Florida
Gainesville, FL

Ms. Deborah M. Harvest
Principal
Johnnie L. Cochran, Jr. Academy
East Orange, NJ

Ms. Lynda E. Irvin
Illinois Gates Coalition
College of Education
Educational Administration and Foundations
Illinois State University
Normal, IL

Ms. Gail S. Karwoski
Principal
Daniels Farm School
Trumbull, CT

Mr. Primus M. Moore
Principal
Eugene Field Elementary School
McAlester, OK

Mr. Daniel Saltrick
Education Consultant
Instructional & Accountability Systems
Cornelius, NC

Ms. Connie Weigleb Sipes
Principal
Fairmont Elementary School
New Albany, IN

Mr. Gregory D. Weatherspoon
Principal
Riddle Elementary School
Lansing, MI

Dr. Edward D. Wiggins
Principal
Carver Middle School
Raymond, MS

Acknowledgements

Developing *Leading Learning Communities: Standards for What Principals Should Know and Be Able To Do* was a collaborative process synthesizing research, personal reflections and collective wisdom. NAESP gratefully acknowledges the people who contributed to this effort, including:

- The many principals — aspiring, new, veteran and retired — who generously shared their stories and whose passion challenges us all to remember the children

- Executive Directors of NAESP State Affiliates and the many principals who serve as State Leaders, for their deep commitment to the work of our professional associations

- James L. Doud, Ph.D., who served as special consultant to the research and development of the project

- Educational Research Service, John M. Forsyth, Ph.D., President, and Joseph D'Amico, Vice-President, for their continuing support and significant contributions to the research and practice of school leadership

- For their insightful review: Joe Schneider, Deputy Executive Director, American Association of School Administrators; Carole Kennedy, National Board for Professional Teaching Standards; Ruth Mitchell, the Education Trust; and George Perry, Perry and Associates

- Collaborative Communications Group, for their shared belief in the process of collaboration and for their tireless commitment to reporting the authentic voice of our nation's school leaders, especially Kris Kurtenbach, President; Terri Ferinde Dunham; Beth Bacon; Liz Worley and Patrick Riccards

- The NAESP staff, for their understanding of the changing role of the principals and their commitment to serving elementary and middle school principals across the country:

Vincent L. Ferrandino, Ed.D., Executive Director; Gail Connelly Gross, Deputy Executive Director; Deborah B. Reeve, Ed.D., Deputy Executive Director; Fred Brown, Associate Executive Director, Professional Services; Cheryl Riggins, Ed.D., Associate Executive Director, Urban Alliances; Ann Walker, Assistant Executive Director, NAESP Leadership Academy; Lee Greene, Assistant Executive Director, Publications/Editorial Services; Margaret Evans, Assistant Executive Director, Community and Student Services; LuAnn Martinson, Assistant Executive Director, Membership/Marketing Services; Ernest J. Mannino, Assistant Executive Director, National Principals Resource Center; Sally McConnell, Ph.D., Director, Government Relations; June Million, Director, Public Information; Merrie Hahn, Director, Programs; Harold Harris, Manager, National Principals Resource Center; Diana Stanley, Executive Assistant, and Erika Lopez-Tello, Administrative Assistant

NAESP also acknowledges the vision, leadership and commitment provided to this project and to the profession by the principals who serve as members of the NAESP Board of Directors:

President
Darrell C. Rud
Newman Elementary School
Billings, MT

President-elect
Paul G. Young
West Elementary School
Lancaster, OH

Past President
Richard F. Barbacane
Buehrle Elementary School
Lancaster, PA

Director, Zone 1
Edward A. Handi
Green Acres Elementary School
North Haven, CT

Director, Zone 2
Mary M. Reece
Menlo Park School
Edison, NJ

Director, Zone 3
Barry S. Band,
Third Ward Elementary School
Elkins, WV

Director, Zone 4
Bruce A. Voelkel
Banyan Elementary School
Sunrise, FL

Director, Zone 5
Rosemarie I. Young
Watson Lane Elementary School
Louisville, KY

Director, Zone 6
Susan Elizabeth Masterson
Monroe Elementary School
Janesville, WI

Director, Zone 7
Marly J. Wilson
Mellette Elementary School
Watertown, SD

Director, Zone 8
Marcia K. Brueggen
Linwood Elementary School
Oklahoma City, OK

Director, Zone 9
Judy A. Thomas
Wilcox Elementary School
Pocatello, ID

Director, Foundation
Anthony Harduar
Central Elementary School
Ferndale, WA

Director, Foundation
Edward J. Jerome
The Edgartown School
Edgartown, MA

Bibliography

STANDARD ONE: BALANCE MANAGEMENT AND LEADERSHIP ROLES

Association of Washington School Administrators. *Principal Leadership in a Performance-Based School.* Olympia, WA: AWSA, March 2001.

Barth, R. *Improving School From Within: Teachers, Parents and Principals Can Make a Difference.* San Francisco: Jossey-Bass, 1990.

Boyer, E. *The Basic School: A Community of Learning.* Princeton, NJ: The Carnegie Foundation for the Advancement of Teaching, 1995.

Doud, J. and E. Keller. *A Ten-Year Study: The K-8 Principal in 1998.* Alexandria, VA: National Association of Elementary School Principals, 1998.

Fink, E. and L. Resnick. "Developing Principals as Instructional Leaders." Vol. 82. No. 9. *Phi Delta Kappan.* Bloomington, IN: Phi Delta Kappa International, April 2001.

Fullan, M. *What's Worth Fighting For in the Principalship?* New York: Teachers College Press, 1997.

Fullan, M. and A. Hargreaves. *What's Worth Fighting For in Your School.* New York: Teachers College Press, 1996.

Gardner, J. *On Leadership.* New York: The Free Press, 1990.

Greenleaf, R. *Servant-Leadership: A Journey Into the Nature of Legitimate Power and Greatness.* New York: Paulist Press, 1977.

Southwest Educational Development Laboratory. "Professional Learning Communities: What Are They and Why Are They Important?" Vol. 6, No. 1. *Issues…about Change*. Austin, TX: Southwest Educational Development Laboratory, 1997.

Kennedy, C. "Splitting the Principalship." Vol. 80, No. 4. *Principal*. Alexandria, VA: National Association of Elementary School Principals, March 2001.

Leithwood, K., D. Jantzi, and R. Steinbach. *Changing Leadership for Changing Times*. Buckingham, UK: Open University Press, 1999.

National Research Council. *How People Learn: Brain, Mind, Experience and School*. Washington, DC: National Academy Press, 2000.

Olson, L. "New Thinking on What Makes a Leader." *Education Week*. January 19, 2000.

Sergiovanni, T. *Leadership for the Schoolhouse: How Is It Different? Why Is It Important?* San Francisco: Jossey-Bass, 1996.

STANDARD TWO: SET HIGH EXPECTATIONS AND STANDARDS

Achieve, Inc. "Giving All Students a Fair Shot." Achieve Policy Brief. Washington, DC: Achieve, Inc., April 2000.

Ackerman, R., G. Donaldson, Jr. and R. Van Der Bogert. *Making Sense As a School Leader: Persisting Questions, Creative Opportunities*. San Francisco: Jossey-Bass, 1996.

Black, S. "Finding Time To Lead." *American School Board Journal*. September 2000.

Blase, J. and J. Blase. *Empowering Teachers: What Successful Principals Do*. Thousand Oaks, CA: Corwin Press, 2000.

Boyer, E. *The Basic School: A Community for Learning*. Princeton, NJ: The Carnegie Foundation for the Advancement of Teaching, 1995.

Deal, T. and K. Peterson. *Shaping School Culture: The Heart of Leadership*. San Francisco: Jossey-Bass, 1998.

Educational Research Service, National Association of Elementary School Principals and National Association of Secondary School Principals. *The Principal, Keystone of a High-Achieving School: Attracting and Keeping the Leaders We Need*. Arlington, VA: ERS, 2000.

Elmore, R. "Building a New Structure for School Leadership." Washington, DC: Albert Shanker Institute, Winter 2000.

Hart (Peter D.) Research Associates. "Standards-Based Education Reform: Teachers' and Principals' Perspectives." Washington, DC: Albert Shanker Institute, September 1999.

Mid-continent Research for Education and Learning. "Standards-Based Accountability Systems." Policy Brief. Aurora, CO: McREL, April 2000.

National Commission on Time and Learning. "Prisoners of Time." Online. 1994. Available: www.ed.gov/pubs/prisonersoftime.

O'Neil, J. "On Schools as Learning Organizations: A Conversation with Peter Senge." Vol. 52. No. 7. *Educational Leadership*. April 1995.

Schlechty, P. *Inventing Better Schools: An Action Plan for Educational Reform*. San Francisco: Jossey-Bass, 1997.

Senge, P. *Schools That Learn: A Fifth Discipline Fieldbook for Educators, Parents and Everyone Who Cares About Education*. New York: Doubleday, 2000.

Sergiovanni, T. *Leadership for the Schoolhouse: How Is It Different? Why Is It Important?* San Francisco: Jossey-Bass, 1996.

Shapiro, N. and J. Levine. *Creating Learning Communities: A Practical Guide to Winning Support, Organizing for Change and Implementing Programs*. San Francisco: Jossey-Bass, 1999.

Silverstein, M. "Snapshot of Standards Implementation in Action." *Connections*. Washington, DC: Public Education Network, Spring 2000.

Southwest Educational Development Laboratory. "Co-Developers: Partners in a Study of Professional Learning Communities." Vol. 8, No. 2. *Issues…about Change*. Austin, TX: Southwest Educational Development Laboratory, 2000.

Southwest Educational Development Laboratory. "Principals and Teachers: Continuous Learners." Vol. 7, No. 2. *Issues…about Change*. Austin, TX: Southwest Educational Development Laboratory, 1999.

WestEd. "Time and Learning: Making Time Count." Policy brief. San Francisco: WestEd, May 2001.

STANDARD THREE: DEMAND CONTENT AND INSTRUCTION THAT ENSURE STUDENT SUCCESS

Barkley, S., et. al. *Leadership Matters: Building Leadership Capacity.* Atlanta: Southern Regional Education Board, April 2001.

Brenner, T. "Perceptions of Students, Parents, and Teachers Toward Cooperative Teaching." Dissertation. University of North Dakota. 1999.

DuFour, R. and R. Eaker. *Professional Learning Communities at Work: Best Practices for Enhancing Student Achievement.* Bloomington, IN: National Educational Service, 1998.

Sanders, W. and Rivers, J. "Cumulative Residual Effects of Teachers on Future Student Academic Achievement." 1998.

STANDARD FOUR: CREATE A CULTURE OF CONTINUOUS LEARNING FOR ADULTS

Blase, J. and J. Blase. *Empowering Teachers: What Successful Principals Do.* Thousand Oaks, CA: Corwin Press, 2000.

Educational Research Service. *Professional Development for School Principals.* Bloomington, IN: National Educational Service, 1999.

Institute for Educational Leadership. *Leadership for Student Learning: Redefining the Teacher as Leader.* Washington, DC: IEL, April 2001.

Girvin, N. *The Principal's Role in K-12 Professional Development.* Washington, DC: Council for Basic Education, May 2001.

Joyce, B. and B. Showers. *Student Achievement Through Staff Development: Fundamentals of School Renewal.* White Plains, NY: Longman Publishing Group, 1995.

Joyce, B., et al. *The New Structure of School Improvement: Inquiring Schools and Achieving Students.* Milton Keynes, UK: Open University, 1999.

National Staff Development Council. *Learning To Lead, Leading To Learn: Improving School Quality Through Principal Professional Development.* Oxford, OH: NSDC, December 2000.

National Staff Development Council. *Standards for Staff Development.* Oxford, OH: NSDC, revised 2001.

New Visions for Public Schools. "Principal Mentoring Program Abstract." 2001. Online: www.newvisions.org/pmp.

Norton, J. "Teachers Get Help From 'Guide on the Side.'" *Changing Schools in Long Beach.* Atlanta: Focused Reporting Project, Fall 1999.

U.S. Department of Education. "Building Bridges: The Mission and Principles of Professional Development." Goals 2000. Online: www.ed.gov/G2K/bridge.html

Wald, P. and M. Castleberry. *Educators as Learners: Creating a Professional Learning Community in Your School.* Alexandria, VA: Association for Supervision and Curriculum Development, 2000.

WestEd. *Teachers Who Learn, Kids Who Achieve: A Look at Schools with Model Professional Development.* San Francisco: WestEd, 2000.

STANDARD FIVE: USE MULTIPLE SOURCES OF DATA AS DIAGNOSTIC TOOLS

American Association of School Administrators. "Data-Driven Decisions: New Ways To Get Answers." No. 4. Vol. 58. *The School Administrator.* Arlington, VA: AASA, April 2001.

Annenberg Institute for School Reform. "Using Data for School Improvement: Report on the Second Practitioners' Conference for Annenberg Challenge Sites." Providence, RI: Brown University, 1998.

Arter, J. and J. McTighe. *Scoring Rubrics in the Classroom: Using Performance Criteria for Assessing and Improving Student Performance.* Thousand Oaks, CA: Corwin Press, 2000.

Carter, S. C. *No Excuses: Lessons from 21 High-Performing, High-Poverty Schools.* Washington, DC: The Heritage Foundation, 2000.

Creighton, T. "Data Analysis in Administrators' Hands: An Oxymoron?" *The School Administrator.* Arlington, VA: AASA, April 2001.

The Education Trust. *Community Data Guide.* Washington, DC: The Education Trust.

Holcomb, E. L. *Getting Excited About Data: How To Combine People, Passion and Proof.* Thousand Oaks, CA: Corwin Press, 1999.

Killion, J. and G. T. Bellamy. "On the Job: Data Analysts Focus School Improvement Efforts," *Journal of Staff Development.* Oxford, OH: National Staff Development Council, Winter 2000.

National Education Association. "Data-Driven Decision Making and Student Achievement." Online: www.nea.org/publiced/standars/dddm.html.

Stiggins, R. *Student-Involved Classroom Assessment.* Upper Saddle River, NJ: Prentice Hall, 2001.

Wiggins, G. P. *Assessing Student Performance: Exploring the Purpose and Limits of Testing.* San Francisco: Jossey Bass. 1993.

STANDARD SIX: ACTIVELY ENGAGE THE COMMUNITY

Annenberg Institute for School Reform. *Reasons for Hope, Voices for Change.* 1998.

The Coalition for Community Schools. "Key Principles of Community Schools" and "Approaches to Community Schools." Washington, DC: Institute for Educational Leadership. Online: www.communityschools.org

Cortes, E., Jr. "Making the Public the Leaders in Education Reform." *Education Week.* November 22, 1995.

Clark, R. M. "Why Disadvantaged Students Succeed." *Connections.* Atlanta: Boys & Girls Club of America, Summer 1992.

Dryfoos, J. *Full-Service Schools: A Revolution in Health and Social Services for Children, Youth and Families.* San Francisco: Jossey-Bass, 1994.

Dryfoos, J. *Safe Passage: Making It Through Adolescence in a Risky Society.* Oxford, UK: Oxford University Press, 1998.

Lemann, N. "Kicking in Groups," *Atlantic Monthly.* April 1996.

Mathews, D. *Is There a Public for Public Schools?* Dayton, OH: Kettering Foundation Press, 1996.

McClure, G. *Shared Decision-Making: The Benefits and the Pitfalls.* ASSA/NAESP/NASSP School-Based Management Task Force. 1992.

Murnane, R. and F. Levy. "What General Motors Can Teach U.S. Schools About the Proper Role of Markets in Education Reform." *Phi Delta Kappan.* Bloomington, IN: Phi Delta Kappa International, October 1996.

National PTA. *Building Successful Partnerships: A Guide for Developing Parent and Family Involvement Programs.* Washington, DC: National Education Service, 2000.

National School Boards Association. *Communities Count: A School Board Guide to Public Engagement.* Alexandria, VA: National School Boards Association, 2000.

National School Boards Association. *The Community Connection: Case Studies in Public Engagement.* Alexandria, VA: National School Boards Association, 2000.

Patrikakou, E., et al. "Positive Communication Between Parents and Teachers." No. 103. *Partnerships.* Philadelphia: Laboratory for Student Success, 1997.

Schorr, L. *Common Purpose: Strengthening Families and Neighborhoods To Rebuild America.* New York: Doubleday, 1997.

Southern Regional Education Board. "Strategy IV, Building Community Collaboration: Partnerships for Improvement." *The SREB Model for Leadership Development.* Atlanta: SREB, 2000.

U. S. Department of Education. "Family Involvement in Children's Education: Successful Local Approaches." Online: www.ed.gov/pubs/FamInvolve.

Van Slyke, S. "Building Community for Public Schools," *Phi Delta Kappan.* Bloomington, IN: Phi Delta Kappa International, June 1997.

Wolk, R. A. "A National Strategy of Public Engagement in the Effort To Improve America's Schools." Providence, RI: Annenberg Institute for School Reform, Fall/Winter 1996.

ADDITIONAL RESOURCES

Bottoms, G. and K. O'Neill. *Preparing a New Breed of School Principals: It's Time for Action.* Atlanta: Southern Regional Education Board, April 2001.

Cotton, K. *Principals of High-Achieving Schools: What the Research Says.* Portland, OR: Northwest Regional Educational Laboratory, March 2001.

Educational Research Service. "Is There a Shortage of Qualified Candidates for Openings in the Principalship?: An Exploratory Study." Arlington, VA: ERS, January 1998.

Elmore, R. "Getting to Scale with Good Educational Practice." Vol. 66. No. 1. *Harvard Education Review.* Cambridge, MA: Harvard University, Spring 1996.

Fullan, M. G. "Turning Systemic Thinking on Its Head." *Phi Delta Kappan.* Bloomington, IN: Phi Delta Kappa International, February 1996.

Hoachlander, G., et al. *Leading School Improvement: What Research Says.* Atlanta: Southern Regional Education Board, March 2001.

Institute for Educational Leadership. *Leadership for Student Learning: Restructuring School District Leadership.* Washington, DC: Institute for Educational Leadership, February 2001.

Interstate School Leaders Licensure Consortium. *Standards for School Leaders.* Washington, DC: Council of Chief State School Officers, 1996.

National Association of Elementary School Principals. "The Principalship in Crisis." Vol. 80. No. 4. *Principal.* Alexandria, VA: NAESP, March 2001.

Parents for Public Schools. "School Leadership: It's About Teaching and Learning." *Parents Press.* Jackson, MS: Parents for Public Schools, December 2000.

Notes/Reflections

Please send me the following publications:

	Quantity	Total
Leading Learning Communities: Standards for What Principals Should Know and Be Able to Do Members: $19.95 Non-members: $24.95 Order #LLC		
After-School Programs and the K-8 Principal: Standards for Quality School-age Child Care (Revised Edition) Members: $14.95 Non-members: $19.95 Order #SACC		
Early Childhood Education and the Elementary School Principal: Standards for Quality Programs for Young Children (Second Edition) Members: $14.95 Non-members: $19.95 Order #ECE		
Essentials for Principals: How to Interview, Hire and Retain High-Quality New Teachers Members: $19.95 Non-members: $24.95 Order #HTI		
Essentials for Principals: School Leader's Guide to Special Education Members: $19.95 Non-members: $24.95 Order #ESE		
Essentials for Principals: Strengthening the Connection between School and Home Members: $19.95 Non-members: $24.95 Order #ESTC		
Essentials for Principals: Meeting the Challenges of High-Stakes Testing Members: $19.95 Non-members: $24.95 Order #EHST		
Essentials for Principals: Data-Based Decision-Making Members: $19.95 Non-members: $24.95 Order #EDBDM		
	Subtotal	
	VA residents add 4.5% sales tax	
	Shipping & Handling Minimum $ 4.50	
	Total Order	

Bill & Ship to: ☐ School ☐ Home

Name _____

School/District/Firm _____

Address _____

City, State, Zip _____

Member ID# (for member price) _____

P.O. Number _____

Charge to:
☐ Bill Me
☐ Visa   ☐ MC   ☐ Am Ex   ☐ Discover

Card # _____

Exp. Date _____   Signature _____

To order by phone, call 1-800-386-2377 or 703-684-3345 To order on-line: www.naesp.org